FLIPPING HOUSES FOR BEGINNERS

Effective Strategies in Buying and Selling Houses

(Quick Start Guide to Investing in Properties)

Brian Hazelwood

Published by Tomas Edwards

Flipping Houses for Beginners: Effective Strategies in Buying and Selling Houses (Quick Start Guide to Investing in Properties)

ISBN 978-1-990373-16-9

Legal & Disclaimer

The information contained in this book is not designed to replace or take the place of any form of medicine or professional medical advice. The information in this book has been provided for educational and entertainment purposes only.

The information contained in this book has been compiled from sources deemed reliable, and it is accurate to the best of the Author's knowledge; however, the Author cannot guarantee its accuracy and validity and cannot be held liable for any errors or omissions. Changes are periodically made to this book. You must consult your doctor or get professional medical advice before using any of the suggested remedies, techniques, or information in this book.

Table of Contents

Introduction

This book contains proven steps and strategies on how to flip houses and make the most from flipping property. If you are looking to learn crucial skills that will help you to attain financial freedom through the practical application of knowledge, then this book is the right choice for you. It is an aggregation of experience from 2 generations of real estate investment gurus. The book is fun and straightforward to read, and it exposes users to technical knowledge.

Buying and selling real estate is a very profitable venture. The concept of buying and selling real estate properties or flipping is one of the surer ways of making money. There are several ways to approach this; whether you buy a property and hold it for years until you can sell it for a higher price, or you do that within days, weeks, or even months.

Perhaps you picked up this book because you are wondering how you can make money from real estate. Many people have built lucrative streams of income by making the most out of their investments in real estate.

How easy is real estate?

I have come across several people that ask me this question before going into real estate.

It isn't easy, because it is easy to fall into the hands of scamming gurus who try to teach about flipping houses with motivational quotes.

Real estate is not a get-rich-quick or some Ponzi scheme. It is a business that requires patience, diligence, and the application of well-defined rules. At the end of this book, you will not only understand these rules, but you will also be exposed to practical applications.

To make the best from real estate, you will need to ensure that you plant the right seeds and subsequently "nourish' these seeds. Real estate can be made accessible when you put in the right amount of effort to ensure that you meet up with your objectives. You need to have a plan if you want to run a real estate investment business successfully.

As a new investor, you are likely eager to get things rolling and start making a killing. This cannot happen by accident, and you need to work with a blueprint or a plan to successfully do this.

Chapter 1: Preparing for Change as

a 9-5 Millennial

Millennials, equally referred to as the Net Generation or Generation Y, consist of a demographic which comes after Generation X. Millennials is a term which is typically used to describe individuals born between 1980 – 2000.

Millennials were raised in a world filled with electronics and connected socially. This generation has attained the most attention from marketing. Because they are the most diverse generation in terms of ethnicity, they are more accepting of differences.

This set of individuals are usually more confident because they were told they were unique. Millennials also have more optimism about America's future in comparison to other generations. This remains the case even though they are the first generation that is expected to attain less economic success in comparison to their parents.

One major result of the optimism many Millennials have is heading into adulthood with unrealistic expectations. Sometimes, this may result in disappointment. Many early Millennials went past post-secondary education only to end up underemployed, in unrelated sectors, or moving between various jobs more regularly than the past generations. Some of them even remain stuck in these dead-end jobs, making other individuals rich instead of engaging in something beneficial to them.

Their expectations may have come from the very involved and encouraging group of parents we call the helicopter parents today.

Presently, the generation of millennials is dealing with issues in the market as opposed to previous generations. Many millennials are battling to survive in the market. With numerous problems ranging from inflation in the education sector, A.I job screening, less earning than past generations, fast growth in technology, dealing with more college debts, and a host of other issues, the millennials don't find it easy as many of these make it even more complicated for them.

However, technology has given Millennials an edge. Many millennials were raised with the internet and computers with a GUI or graphical user interface. Because they are familiar with all of these, they have a less stressful time understanding visual languages and interfaces. They can adjust quickly to new OS or operating systems, devices, and programs. They are equally more capable of performing tasks that are computer-based faster than in past generations. Although there is proof that multitasking is not an efficient manner of working, Millennials could be the employees that can make it work.

Generally, Millennials don't have issues with the concept of public internet life. From the perspective of the Millennial, privacy is mostly an issue of functional setting that limits who can see what they share online. The level of comfort they have with social media implies that they are great at promoting themselves and great at creating connections via social media.

However, this approach often leads to a problem when they compare themselves with their peers. When it has to do with getting things done, Millennials depend on the internet a lot. If any issue arises with their devices or gadgets, they often head to the internet to look for help in pointing out and correcting these problems.

All of these ensures that this generation has a more in-depth understanding of hardware issues and programming all of which gives them an edge in the current market. One of the edges millennials have with their knowledge of the internet and getting things done is that, they can engage in various kinds of businesses right from the comfort of their homes. This is possible without the need to go into the continuous cycle of the 9-5. A perfect example of this is the business of flipping houses. With their knowledge of technology and the way the internet works, they can be one of the leaders in the business in no time.

The Lie of the 9-5

Speaking frankly, the standard 9-5 job to help someone achieve his/her goals is not fun. You spend all your time working for another individual with minimal freedom. As if that is not enough, the cash you make is not proportional to the amount of work you are putting in.

The great news is that, there are other things you can do which would help you earn all the cash you need without having to compromise your freedom and well-being. One of these is the business of flipping houses. If you go into the business of flipping, you can be your own boss, work during your free time and still remain fulfilled in the process.

But knowing this, why then are a lot of individuals okay with working the 9-5? Let us check out the common misconceptions that encourage this:

Sense of Security

For many individuals, working 9-5 offers them a sense of security knowing they would always get an income within a specific period of the month. This results in people becoming comfortable waiting for that period of the month when their salary comes in.

However, this can't be further from the truth. In a 9-5 job, you only have a false sense of security because your stay the next day is not absolute. It only takes a minor issue to make you lose your job and be left with nothing. If you are told your services are no longer required, you have no other option than to leave, losing that sense of security you cherish.

Set Work Hours

For many people, knowing the set period they would work is refreshing. They understand that after the set 9-5, they are free to do whatever they want and thrive on this. They just work all day and head out when the clock hits 5 pm.

Again, this is another false belief. In many organizations, work goes past the set 5 pm. Numerous times, you even go home with some paperwork depending on your profession. Additionally, the set work period makes it a bit rigid. For instance, if your child needs you during work hours or an emergency arises, depending on your kind of job, you may not be able to leave.

Capacity to Plan Properly

Because of the set 9-5, many people believe they can make proper plans. They know when they would be busy at work and make plans after work hours.

It's not easy to plan all your activities after 5 pm which is the typical closing time. You may end up missing out on a range of family events which typically take place earlier, and it could be strenuous on both you and your family.

Those are just a few misconceptions people have which makes them remain in 9-5 jobs. However, these jobs are harming you in more ways than you know.

Below are some issues you may deal with if you stay in a 9-5 job.

You Don't Feel Fulfilled

This is very common for most people. Many people are stuck in jobs they never wanted in the first place, either as a means to earn a living or because their parents decided their paths.

You now have the job you desired, and you have a lot of cash. But are you fulfilled? You need to be in a job that you are passionate about and excites you.

Many 9-5 jobs are repetitive and so draining because you wake, rush off to work, head back home and repeat the process once more. It can be a very unfulfilling way to live.

You Are Wasting Valuable Time

Right now, you are likely within the ages of 18 to 60. Your frustrating alarm wakes you up every day. You hit the snooze button numerous times hoping you could just relax today. You know it is impossible and finally, you get up and head to work.

You drag yourself to work where you get to your desk. You will remain here for the next 8 hours. Time seems to be slow, but eventually, it hits 5pm, and you get to go home. Then you realize you have to repeat this process tomorrow and yes, you do the same thing again, until you are in your 60s and almost depressed. For many people, this is not the case, but for a lot of people, this is how it usually goes.

However, you need to note that this time you spent is something you can never get back. It is gone forever. You could have used it in achieving something for yourself instead of someone else.

That is not all. Many individuals are starting to put in more work hours as a result of more bills to be paid among a host of other reasons. You find out that the time you have to yourself is dwindling even more.

Working longer does not mean you would get rich overnight. Instead, it is a terrible idea especially if you plan on achieving any goal for yourself. If you want to achieve your goals and make something of yourself, you need to let go of the 9-5 mindset.

How Can You Do This?

You need to take a step today. There are many things you can try out that would be more fulfilling than taking a 9-5 job.

Don't get me wrong; there is no perfect job out there. You still face a lot of issues if you decide to do your own thing. It comes with a higher reward, but the risks are also high. You won't get any bonuses, raises, or benefits each year. You won't get a paycheck during a stipulated period. However, the potential advantages are way more than the negatives. You need to make that bold move today, and you would have no regrets in the end.

Mindset Madness

A good number of us remain stuck in our present life situation as a result of fear. This is something that comes for a reason. As a species, we have been able to survive with the help of fear. However, that tool that has helped us survive may also be what is keeping you stuck in an unpleasant life situation.

Many of us do not move forward due to many reasons beyond the fear of failure. When we come across the possibility to fail, many of us decide to remain safe and stay where we are as opposed to exposing ourselves to the possibility of failure.

If you want to move forward and get out of your present life situation, you must identify those fears which are preventing you from taking action. Once you do this, you can then deal with them.

Below are some of the characteristics that you would require if you want to achieve this. They are:

Positive Mindset

Your mindset is a collection of beliefs and thoughts that aid in shaping the way you think. Your thought habits have an impact on what you feel, what you do, and the way you think. Your mindset also has an impact on how you see yourself and how you see the world. Your mindset is a huge deal, and if you plan of getting out of your present life situation, it is the first thing you need to work on.

What you channel your mind to is the location you will automatically channel your action to. You need to try to stay positive and believe in yourself the best way you can. A few of the top ways of doing this is to surround yourself with inspiring and positive individuals, write down the progress you have made, and start listening to motivational and positive materials.

15

Cultivate Grit

You need to be passionate about anything you plan on doing. In this situation, it is the goal you want to achieve, to leave your present life situation. This will ensure the persistence to see it to the end.

Having an in-depth interest in what you want to do is one of the crucial things that will help you stay motivated. If you want to accomplish your goals of leaving your present situation, you need to have the determination to ensure you stay on the right path.

Patience

Patience is not the same as waiting. Waiting does not involve action. By practicing patience, you continue working toward your goals even when the results are not visible yet. If you are waiting without doing any work, you have stopped. Patience means believing in your goal enough to ensure it keeps you moving forward.

Accountability

You need to be responsible for your inner and external life which include your actions, feelings, and thoughts. This is an essential trait to develop. It means you take responsibility for the results of your actions. If you can admit your errors and face the facts while knowing it does not reduce your worth, then you are on the right path to learning accountability.

Self-Confidence

To get past your comfort zone and move further in life, self-confidence is a crucial trait you need. It has to do with your willingness to explore new areas, leave your present situation, take risks, and dive into new things.

The significant part of self-confidence is that you can fake it till you make it. You may have many doubts and fears before you do something, but you will still be able to project confidence, even if you don't have it yet. One of the best ways of developing confidence is to believe that you have what it requires to deal with any uncertainty that may come your way when you take that step forward.

Habit vs. Mindset

Have you ever imagined why it sometimes feels like a battle to get ahead? The reality is that if you want to be successful at what you do, you need to have a high level of discipline in your mindset. The reason is simple; your mindset has a way of affecting your habits.

If, in your mind, you believe that you cannot change a bad habit, then you will never make any effort to correct it. You will stay away from situations that you believe are uncomfortable and may not get anywhere close to your goal.

So what are the habits you need to pick up if you want to achieve success in whatever you are doing and how do you correct your mindset into changing them?

Let's take a look at some ways to do this below:

Let Go of the Fixed Mindset

Individuals who have a fixed mindset believe that talents and habits are traits you cannot change. They also believe that to be successful, all you need is to be talented without making any effort. This is not true.

Successful individuals are aware of this. They channel a lot of time every day in developing a growth mindset, changing how they see things, and learning new skills to improve their lives.

Don't forget that the person you are now, does not have to be who you are tomorrow.

Acknowledge Your Flaws

Perhaps you procrastinate a lot and end up doing things in a rush at the last minute. You can tailor your plans around that. Make reasonable goals and give yourself adequate time to achieve them.

Understand Your Style of Learning

If you can point out the easiest ways for you to learn, you can effectively use your time when trying to achieve a goal. This will let you work using various patterns that work for you, making you achieve goals faster.

Don't Forget That Learning Requires Time

Anything worth doing takes time. You need to be realistic regarding the time it will require for you to achieve the goal you want. You need to move a little step forward each day, but eventually, you are guaranteed to get to your destination.

Are You Ready To Move Forward?

If you want to develop great habits, you need to be ready to change your mindset about the things you can do and the habits you already have. You cannot obstruct your progress with the notion that there is no room for you to change those habits that are not of benefit to you.

You need to take the needed actions to learn, remain motivated and take little steps every day for you to be successful. By determining what works for you and dropping habits that are drawing you back, you will be able to learn great lessons and achieve success in all aspects of your life.

Investing In Yourself by Investing In House Flipping

Most times, when you hear about investment, it is usually about investing money. However, most of these fail to mention that you can equally invest in yourself. Doing this will ensure you make returns that would last through your entire life.

Do you know that you can invest in yourself by investing in house flipping? The possibilities are limitless. The question is, how exactly do you achieve this? That is what we will be covering in this section.

Invest In Your Mind

By investing in your mind, it means you need to read and obtain information concerning house flipping and things that you need to know before investing. You need to understand the basics and find out the core information. All of these will ensure you are ready before you invest.

You Can Earn Continuous Income from Rent Before You Sell

When you invest in a house flipping business, even if you are unable to sell a property, you will be able to earn continuous income via this business. You can re-channel some of the income into the upgrade and maintenance of your property. All of these are expenses which would amount to nothing when you consider the revenue you can get from real estate. Eventually, when you sell the property, it would have probably risen in value, which would bring you additional revenue.

You Are Protected From the Volatile Market

When you begin a house flipping business, you don't have to deal with the market volatility that Wall Street faces. In the stock market, a bear market can quickly clear out a massive chunk of your financial portfolio. However, in the business of house flipping, these forces are not applicable. By going into a house flipping business, you are going into a secure and stable real estate investment that is going to increase in value with time.

The instant you begin a house flipping business, you join a group of individuals who live conveniently off a reliable and stable investment. To attain success, the important thing is to know that you are investing in a steady income source which you would benefit from down the road. By investing in the house flipping business, you automatically invest in yourself which would be way more beneficial in the long run.

Chapter 2: What You Need To Get

Started

So you have decided that you want to undertake your first house-flipping project. Before you rush out and find a house to flip, be sure you have all the tools you need to start out strong. There are two sets of requirements you should consider: essentials and specifics. Essential requirements involve your mentality and perspective about house-flipping, while specific requirements get down to brass tax and numbers. You will need both when beginning your first house flip. The essentials

1. Time

House-flipping takes time. Though it is a relatively quick process (ideally), you have to find time to get the house, fix the house, and then sell the house. If you have a full-time job already, this means filling your free time and weekends with the flipping project. If you don't have time and cannot make time for a house flip, you shouldn't do it. The longer you take to get the house ready and sold, the more money it costs you.

2. Money

Speaking of money, this is the second essential. Even if you are able to buy a house wholesale and pay less than you would otherwise on your flip house, you need money for repairs, taxes, and so on. Experts recommend a cushion, so you have a bit more flexibility when unexpected expenses pop up.

3. Knowledge

When you flip a house, you need to know what you're doing. This includes an understanding of the real estate market, house ownership, taxes, and construction. You can accumulate knowledge through reading, talking to people, and first-hand experience with making repairs, owning a home, and so on.

4. Ability to problem-solve

Being able to problem-solve is hugely important when you are flipping a house. It is inevitable that something will not go the way as planned, and you will need to figure out a new plan. An inspector might discover a problem that takes longer to fix than anticipated or a contractor might not work out and you have to find one on short notice.

5. Patience

It might take a while to find the perfect house to flip. Don't just buy whatever you see first and what costs the least amount of money. Those extremely cheap houses typically require a ton of repairs, which means more money and a longer construction time. Once you have the house you want, never sacrifice quality for a quick turn-around. This means having the patience to find the best contractor you can and not just getting the first person who comes along. You want your flipped house to sell fast, yes, but you also want to be able to sell it for a high price. The specifics

1. Knowledge about the area your flip is in

Having a firm idea about what the market trends are and what kinds of neighborhoods are most desirable is vital before you buy a house. If you buy a super cheap place in a bad neighborhood, you're going to have a lot of trouble selling it, especially for a good price. Buyers are always told, "Location, location, location," so you need to be aware of info like crime stats, nearby schools, future development plans, and what other houses are selling for in the area.

2. Knowledge about construction

If you've never fixed a leaky sink in your life, taking on a full house renovation is extremely risky. Unless you plan on paying someone else to do all the work (which some flippers do), you need to have a good idea about repairs, power tools, and so on. Most people who want to go into house-flipping do have construction skills and experience. Physically fixing up a house is often one of the things they're most excited about, so odds are you have some idea about what you're doing. If you come across a problem you aren't familiar with, it's important to be humble enough to admit it and not try to mess with it yourself. Issues with electricity can be especially dangerous, so use caution.

3. The right house

The next specific you need before beginning a house-flip project is the actual house. Once you've decided on a good area, you can significantly narrow down your options. The next chapter will go into more detail about how to find a house and what to look for, but for now, just know that choosing the right house to flip makes all the difference in your success or failure. You don't want to get a house that's too cheap that ends up requiring thousands of dollars in repairs, and you don't want one that's too expensive that results in a low profit. Like Goldilocks, you want to find something that's "just right."

4. The right people

If you don't have firsthand knowledge of construction or crunching numbers, you need to build a team who does. A good team could include a real estate estimator, a contractor, house inspector, and anyone else who could fill in gaps. Don't go with the first person you find, or a friend who will do the job for cheap. You want people who have experience, integrity, and an understanding of the risks associated with house-flipping.

5. Specific costs

Having the money for a house-flip is one thing - you will also need to know the specific costs of purchasing a house, repairs, taxes, fees, and so on. You also need to be able to calculate what your profit is going to be, so you go into a house flip knowing what is at stake. Having just a general idea of costs is not enough, you need to have precise budgets and estimates laid out. As mentioned in the "essentials" section above, a cash cushion is valuable for if (or arguably when) unexpected expenses - usually during the repair process - pop up. Experts say to add 20% to your final expensive estimate. If you're on a tight budget, this cushion prevents you from having to scramble for funding or settle for low quality.

Chapter 3: Do Your Math!

There is a lot of math involved with budgeting and house flipping. If you skip over the math, your entire budget will fall apart. Here we will go over everything you need to take into consideration when planning your budget. There are many resources online to help you figure your numbers out. Many will do the math for you! Here are all the calculations you will need when planning your budget.

ARV (After-Rehab Value)- This is one of the most important numbers you will use. This is the amount that you will ultimately sell the house for. You can determine this before buying by looking at what other houses have sold for in your market. That is your goal ARV and can be used when making your budget before even purchasing a house.

Your rehab should stay within 10%-20% of your budget.

MAO (Maximum Allowed Offer)- This is your second most important number. This is how much you can spend to purchase a property.

Here we use the 70% rule. This rule will help you stay within your budget, maximize your profit and reduce risk. First, take your ARV and multiply it by 70% (.70). Subtract your rehab costs and overhead and ta-da! You have your MAO. Now you know how much you can spend on purchasing a property.

Cost of living- This is how much it will cost to maintain the house until it is sold. This includes basic utilities such as water, gas, electric etc. On average this will probably cost $200-$300 a month. That's why it's important to purchase a house you can fix and sell as quickly as possible.

Property Tax (Residential Tax)- These are the yearly taxes you will pay either quarterly or yearly.

Interest on your loan/mortgage- Of course there is interest on your mortgage as with all loans. This is usually based of your credit score and the percentage can be figured daily, monthly or annually.

Mortgage Insurance Premium- If you did not put at least 20% down on your property you will have to pay a mortgage insurance premium (1.75% of your loan amount) as well. (This is used by all FHA-backed lenders on large loans.) The FHA puts this in place to protect the lender in the event of a default on the loan.

Commission- If you hire a realtor (and you absolutely should) you will have to pay a commission, normally once the house is sold.

Closing costs- You will have to pay closing costs twice. First when you purchase the house which is usually between 2%-5% then when you sell the house you will probably pay around 8%.

Capital Gain Tax- When you sell your house, you will have to pay a one-time tax on your profit which is usually about 10%-15%. It is good to factor in your estimation of this though you won't have an actual number until you sell the property.

You are probably wondering how you are supposed to figure all these numbers out before you have even bought a house. You can do your budget before you even get your loan. Using some data from the internet and simple math you can figure this out on your own. By comparing stats on what we call "comp" (comparable) houses, you can determine your budget and what potential your house must sell for. This formula will help you determine your ARV (After Renovation Value) and asking price. Let's break it down.

Step One: Find your comps

A "comp" is a house that is similar to your flip house in a multitude of ways. Using a radius of ½ mile, find two or three homes that are similar in age, style (modern or traditional), condition, amenities and size. Your comps should be within 10% of the same finished square footage and have the same amount of bedrooms, bathrooms, etc. You can easily search for comps on the internet as many websites like Zillow and Trulia do practically all the work for you. You will input some information you are looking for and do a search then narrow your choices down to the 2-3 that are most comparable to yours and go from there.

Step Two: Renovations

Since you have your purchase price, you will now need to figure out how much you are going to spend on renovations. Since we are staying within 10%-20% of your purchase price, if we buy a house for $50,000 that means we are probably going to spend between $5,000-$10,000 on renovations. This includes both materials and labor. You always want to err on the side of caution. If you don't end up spending as much money as you budgeted for then great! But you don't want to budget on the lower end of the spectrum and end up screwing yourself over when you sell.

Step 3: Time is money

So now you are looking an initial price tag of $60,000 for your house. That doesn't sound so bad. However, this is where it can get a bit tricky. The next estimates depend on time. If you estimate for 3 months of time from purchase to sale, but end up spending 5 months on the renovations or the house takes longer to see, these numbers can change. By playing around with the formulas we are about to play with you will be able to see just exactly how much money your time costs. Again, leave yourself wiggle room. Always overestimate.

You will need to add up the cost of utilities, property taxes, insurance and interest. Let's say you are planning on three months of renovations and utilities to run the house are probably going to be about $200, that gives you $600 in utilities.

If your property taxes will be at 1% that means you will be paying $600 a year. By dividing this number by 12 (months in a year) you come to $50 a month. Multiply that by the three months you plan on holding the house and you are looking at $150 in taxes for that time.

Last, we calculate your loan interest. If you took out a loan for $60,000 and your interest rate is at 4%, by multiplying those numbers together you find that you will be paying $2,400 a year in interest. Again, divide this by 12 (months) which gets you $200 per month. Multiply by our 3 months of holding and you have your interest for that period which is $600.

Add all your numbers up now and you will have $71,350 which will cover all your costs and how much you have put into the house. So now let's use the 70% rule to determine your asking price.

Since you're already looking at comp houses, it is worth the time to look at the houses that are not selling in your chosen neighborhood. You may discover houses that are overpriced, outdated or have other issues. Take note of these houses as you can learn what not to do from them. If the higher priced houses have been sitting for months or even years then it should be pretty clear to you where your target asking price is going to be. You might also discover that your neighborhood isn't so popular. If comp houses aren't being sold then it's probably because that area is undesirable and you should probably look elsewhere for a good market.

Looking at this list can be intimidating but don't let it scare you. Here are some tips to help get your budget airtight.

Hire a good CPA (Certified Public Accountant)! He will crunch your numbers and help you build and stay within your budget. He will also be doing your taxes of course so you want to make sure that he has a lot of experience with property taxes, mortgage loans, etc. Again, it is a good idea to ask around to find your CPA.

Ask real estate agents and other house flippers who they use or recommend.

Make sure you get estimates from your contractor in writing so he doesn't increase the price once he begins the work which is an alarmingly common practice.

Hire and consult with your realtor to determine your ARV and estimated taxes. When choosing a realtor, make sure you do your research. Read client reviews, sales numbers, etc. to choose the best one for the job.

Shop around. Get multiple estimates from contractors to make sure you are getting the best deal.

Put down at least 20% if you can to avoid FHA insurance (Mortgage Insurance Premium) and shrink your loan. The less you can borrow is better.

If you follow these steps and are diligent with your budget, your finances will work for you.

Chapter 4: Taxes And Implications

In general, housing reversals are not considered a passive investment by IRS. The tax rules define flipping as "active income" and the profits of the flipped house are treated as regular income with a tax rate of 10% to 37%, not a capital gain of 0% to 20%. The Taxes on house reversals usually include self-employment taxes.

If an investor is classified as a "dealer" by the IRS, the profit from the real estate flip is taxed at the normal income tax rate. Profit is calculated by subtracting the cost, including the purchase price from the final sale price. Tax rates for "active investors" who are earning positive profits range from 10% to 37%.

According to the IRS, property dealers purchase property and sell it to customers "in the normal course of business or business." Most fixed investors are considered dealers.

They hold assets in the short term, and most of their income comes from turning the house over. Even real estate investors who occasionally turn over their homes are usually considered dealers and are taxed at their normal income rate.

On the contrary, profits from real estate held over 12 months are usually subject to more favorable long-term capital gain brackets in the range of 0% to 20%. Investors can choose to rent or occupy the asset.

Normal Income Tax Results When Turning the House Over

If classified as a dealer, the profit from the flip is taxed at the normal rate of income. Currently, the normal income tax rate is 10% to 37%. In addition, profits are subject to self-employment tax (equivalent to self-employed FICA). This is 15.3%, twice the amount normally paid for W2 employees.

As a dealer, Flip's total tax ranges from a minimum of 25.3% to a maximum of 52.3%, depending on the tax rate.

Needless to say, you don't want to misunderstand that your interests are completely yours.

When Capital Gains Tax Applies To Flipping Houses

By avoiding the dealer definition and fortunately gaining from selling the house after turning the house upside down most of year after year, the profit from the sale is taxed at a low capital gain rate.

Note that this is rare for most flippers. Most of the time, they are taxed at the normal income tax rate, but I would like to mention that it happens. Even better, if you are eligible for capital gains tax, you do not have to pay self-employment tax.

Short-Term Capital Gains House Flipping Tax

If the property is held for less than 12 months, there will be no incentive for profits from Flip. Short-term capital gains are taxed at the normal income tax rate, whether defined as a dealer or an investor. However, there is an advantage

42

of not paying 15.3% self-employment tax, so you can still save a lot.

Long-Term Capital Gain House Flipping Tax

If the asset is held for more than one year and is not classified as a dealer, the profit from the flip is taxed according to the long-term capital gain rate. Currently, these tax rates range from 0% to 20% for most taxpayers. Compared to a normal income tax rate and a one-to-two punch of self-employment tax, you can save a lot.

How to Calculate Taxes For Inverted Houses

Eventually, you will be taxed on fixed-price profits. This is the selling price minus total costs and deductions. Profit is calculated by subtracting the cost, including the purchase price from the final sale price.

Purchase Amount

The purchase price includes the cost of the house itself. Although closing expenses, points, etc. may be considered part of the purchase price, to make accounting easier, it is best to treat everything except the actual purchase of the building itself as expenses.

When considering what your profits are, consider only the purchase price, not the amount financed in the profit equation. IRS does not consider funding when calculating profits. However, you can deduct interest paid as expenses.

Expense

Expenses that exceed the purchase price include mortgage interest and points, loan fees, materials and supplies, labor, closure costs, taxes, professional services, and all marketing and real estate agent fees associated with the sale of real estate. The

As the purchase price, the IRS is not worried about how to pay for the costs. As long as the cost is related to the asset, it is usually deductible. For example, if you charge $ 10,000 to a building materials lows credit card, it is considered a property renovation fee.

Home Repair and Turnover Costs

Profit

Profit is the amount settled on sale after all costs, including purchase price have been taken into account. you can put yourself in a better position by having a good record of your expenses to ensure you deduct all renovation expenses. The basic formula is Transaction profit = sale price-purchase price-cost.

Remember when calculating your profits to report that the IRS may not be your actual profits. For example, if you have to repay a mortgage loan that you used to raise funds for purchases and refurbishment, you'll end up with takeaway funds. This amount can be estimated using the following formula: Selling price-Mortgage-Expense = Bringing home profit to investors

Annual Tax

From there, multiplying the taxable income by the normal income tax rate will result in an estimated annual tax burden. Keep in mind that you can use other corrections and flip losses completed in the same year to offset the profit.

How to submit and pay your home to turn over taxes

After calculating the flipping house tax, you need to know when to submit and how to pay. In general, if you are registered as a sole proprietor, part of LLC, or company S, and the home turning business makes more than $ 1,000 a year, you must pay quarterly taxes.

If you haven't generated any revenue or meet other exemptions, you'll report taxes at the end of the year. However, most home flips pay quarterly taxes. These quarterly taxes are known as estimated taxes and are usually paid by April 15, June 15, September 15, and January 15 each year.

For example, if you turn your house over from January 1st to March 31st, your income is April 15th. However, if these dates fall on weekends or holidays, you will be taxed for the next business day.

How to Save House Flipping Tax

While it is difficult to avoid the basic considerations of flipping as an active income, there are some special cases that are not subject to the usual income tax and that help to flip property. These include continuing to invest for longer periods and owning property as your primary residence.

Here Are Few Ways To Reduce Taxes When Turning The House Over.

Holding Investment Property for More Than 1 Year

If you find yourself in a category that can pay capital gains tax instead of regular income tax, predict whether retaining the property for over a year will work. Please note that if you own more than one year, you will be charged a long-term capital gain tax, not a short-term.

Make the Main Residence Before Overturning The Property

If a property is casually turned over, consider whether you can move into that property as your primary residence after the renovation is complete. Moving to real estate may change the tax considerations for the final sale from active income to capital gains. In addition, current tax laws may completely avoid taxing profits if you live in this property for two of the five years prior to sale.

Perform A Tax Postponed Exchange of Flip

The tax deferral exchange, also known as the 1031 exchange, allows you to carry the profits of one property to another property. To qualify for this, you must hold a property for at least one year (which is better from an IRS perspective) and lease it to a tenant. It cannot be used only with the Quick Turn property.

Billing House Flipping Tax Credit

IRS allows house flippers to amortize certain costs associated with the purchase, renovation, and sale of real estate. Offsetting these costs helps reduce taxable income. You can deduct some costs before switching properties, but you cannot deduct other costs, such as capital expenditure until the property is sold.

Costs That Can Be Deducted When Turning Over the House

It is important to know the costs that can be deducted when turning the house over. This will tell you how much your taxable income will be, so you can secure money to pay taxes. This will affect your budget for your next flip.

Costs That Can Be Deducted When Turning The House Upside Down Include:

Capital expenditure (expenses related to buying and refurbishing a house to be turned over). These are subtracted after inverting the properties.

Vehicle costs. This includes gasoline and repair costs, or standard mileage.

Office expenses including rent, utility charges, office supplies such as printer ink and paper

Building permit

Mortgage interest

TYPES OF REAL ESTATE FINANCING

Acquiring the right type of loan can increase purchasing power, ultimately increase cash flow, and increase return on investment. However, borrowers can easily be overwhelmed because there is a variety of real estate lending options to select, investigate, and evaluate from literally thousands of lenders.

So what are the common options for real estate finance? Which option is best for you? Below are some ways to configure real estate transactions and examples of when to use them.

Conventional Loan

If you move into a house that doesn't need repairs and you have fair credit, a traditional loan is a good choice.

Traditional mortgages consider the following information about the borrower:

Credit score

Assets

income

debt

Buyers usually need to pay a down payment of five to twenty-five percent of the purchase price. Traditional loans must meet strict guidelines (as set by investment giants Fannie Mae and Freddie Mac) before being issued. However, borrowers typically benefit from low-interest rates because the risks associated with traditional loans are low.

Blanket Loan

Builders and property developers often look for these loans as an alternative to individual loans for land parcels or multiple properties. Comprehensive loans are used to fund multiple real estates, larger lands, or land that are ultimately segmented and sold. A comprehensive loan allows the borrower to sell a portion of the property without retiring the entire mortgage.

Portfolio Loan

Those who struggle to meet the stringent requirements closely associated with traditional loans can rely on portfolio lenders. Anyone who purchases real estate that doesn't have an acceptable credit rating or does not meet the criteria of the category can consider this option.

A portfolio loan is a mortgage held in a bank portfolio. They are not sold in the secondary market and does not need to comply with underwriting guidelines set by secondary market investors. Portfolio lenders are more flexible in terms of portfolio loan terms but often charge higher interest rates. Portfolio loans are ideal for borrowers who are outside the scope of standard mortgage underwriting guidelines.

Hard Money Loan

Hard money loans are often used to purchase real estate that has poor conditions and requires repair. Unlike traditional mortgages, hard money loans are supported by private funds from individuals or funds from wealthy investors.

Requirement regulations are relaxed, so hard money loans can be protected quickly. Many real estate investors are looking for large loans for a quick turnaround. The lender agrees to do the transaction based on the value of the property, not the buyer's credit, debt, income, assets.

These types of loans are ideal for real estate flippers and other investors but can be expensive. The interest rate of hard money loans is very high compared to conventional loans. It is important to have a strategy on how to terminate a hard money loan and plan to secure a long-term loan at a low-interest rate after a certain period of months.

Piggy Bank

This type of real estate finance, sometimes referred to as a "piggyback" or combo (combo) loan, can be used when the borrower does not pay the full twenty percent required to avoid paying private mortgage insurance (PMI) .

Also, wealthy clients can be used to maintain the first mortgage under the restrictions of Fannie Mae and Freddie Mac to avoid jumbo interest rates. The buyer must pay fifteen percent of the purchase price and split the remainder into a first mortgage with eighty percent of the price and a second mortgage with five percent of the price.

The second number represents the second mortgage, and the third number represents the down payment.

FINANCING OPTION SUMMARY

Financing Types	Loan Amounts	Interest Rates	Repayment Terms	Turnaround Time	Credit Criteria

SBA Loans	$50,000 – $5 million	6% – 13%	5 – 25 years	30 days – 6 months	Usually requires a minimum business credit score (FICO SBSS)
Traditional Bank Loans	$250,000 +	5% – 10%	1 – 20 years	2 – 4 months	Usually requires strong personal and/or business ess

					credit scores
Online Loans	$25,000 – $500,000	7% – 30%	1 – 5 years	2 – 7 days	Less important, but still a main factor
Micro-Loans	$500 – $50,000	8% – 15%	1 -5 years	1 – 3+ months	Less important, but still a main factor
Merchant Cash	$200 – $250	15% – 150	3 – 12 mont	1 – 7 days	Not requi

Advance	,000	%	hs		red
Cash Flow Loans	$200 – $100,000	25% – 90%	6 – 12 months	Minutes – 3 days	Less important, but still a factor
Business Credit Cards	$250 – $25,000	13% 25%	30 days	1 – 3 weeks	Personal and/or business credit are a main factor.
Vendor	$1,000 –	0 –	10 – 120	Hours to	Usually

Finan cing	$100 ,000	36%	days	weeks	requi res good busin ess credit score s

TIPS FOR SUCCESSFUL BORROWING

So you need the money, and you are thinking about asking for a loan for your flipping business here are tips before asking for a loan.

Analyze If You Really Need It

Asking money from either a relative or a bank is nothing that should be taken lightly. Remember that when you ask for money, the ideal is to return it and even with interest, so try to analyze if before reaching that option you have others.

Investigate All Options

Many people, when asking for a loan the first thing they do is go to their favorite bank and take it directly from there, without first evaluating other options. Before requesting a loan you investigate what other banks can offer you, or even look for different ways.

Nowadays, you can apply for loans online, on different platforms, so there are no excuses to investigate and learn more before making any decision.

Try To Look For a Fixed Rate

I never liked the variable word very much. It's true, and it may vary down, but what if he did it up. If possible, try to ask for a fixed-rate loan, so you really know the amount you will be paying each month, and you will not get any other surprises along the way.

Be Careful With the Deadline

Let's assume you are going to ask for a loan for a venture. Then you should keep in mind that the term for the loan payment is not less than the time in which you expect your venture to work.

Otherwise, you will reach that deadline and possibly without having completed the payments as you should.

Have All the Papers Up To Date

Many people at the time of requesting a loan, begin to catch up with their papers to discover that finally, the process becomes delinquent, bureaucratic and even expensive because sometimes you have to take out certain roles that we did not know.

Chapter 5: House Value

You will need to do a lot of studying if you want to get the market just right. For example, we have already explained about a buyer's market and a seller's market. What you also need to know is how quickly houses are shifting in the area where you are thinking of buying a house and the kind of prices that are realized. It pays to look at what is being offered in the area because if you can't compete, then the house is not worth buying.

The best areas to look for properties that are foreclosed are those areas which are highly desirable – where there is an established reputation and demand. Occasionally, you find the odd house which is within that belt and you are able to not only do the work, but up the price to give you a wonderful profit, but you do need to study in advance. Since there are others in the same market as you, that means being very aware of your facts so that when that potential bargain comes up for sale, you are able to pull figures together quickly and make a good solid prediction of how much profit you can expect to make on the property.

So what affects house value?

You can guarantee that a house is put on the market at an optimistic rate. People want to make as much money as is possible. However, there are real pointers to whether you can put in a cheeky offer. For example, have the owners moved on? Are they no longer invested in that particular house? Has the house been on the market for an extended period of time? Has the price been reduced and when was it reduced? If it was only reduced last week, it's hardly likely that a potential seller will be willing to reduce the price even more within such a short space of time. However, if he is no longer invested in the house and the house really hasn't shifted in six months, there's a good chance that you can talk him into an advantageous deal.

The things that will affect the house value will be the condition of the house, the state of the market in that geographical area and the potential cost of trying to get that house back up to a marketable condition. Beware though – because your inspection may not reveal everything. As soon as you start to rip out dry wall, there could be all kinds of hidden horrors so you do need to make sure that you have a contingency fund to deal with things such as this. Thus, if all of your quotations from tradesmen come to £120,000, add $30,000 to your cost because that will help to cover you should anything be discovered that you didn't know about when you bought the house.

You also need to be aware of short sales and sales that are going on in your area which involve repossessions by the bank, or foreclosures as they are well known. In these cases, it's useful to keep yourself appraised of information because there really is a lot of money to be made from this type of home. The thing is that the owner has failed to pay a loan to the bank and the bank are selling the house to recoup their potential loss. That means that a house with a value of $150,000 can actually sell for anything from $80,000 plus because that may be all that is owed to the bank. These are the houses to look out for but as these are relatively quick sales, you also need to have your team on hand, so that you can make an accurate assessment of the potential profit you can make on the house, once it has been renovated and put back on the market at today's prices for that area.

The value of house should always be brought into the equation because if you pay too much and the repairs turn out to be expensive, you could be in for a loss. That's why the next chapter is very important. It shows you the second step which is getting hold of all of the useful contacts that you can so that you have assessments of work prices at hand and can easily make a calculation as to whether the house is worth buying.

Other houses that may sell cheaply are auction houses where the owner or the bank wants a quick return. However, if you are going to buy at auction, you will need to have your finances already in place for the auction date and should make sure that you have researched the house and the area in advance of the sale. You don't get as much time to do your homework but if you have all of your tradesmen sorted out and have done everything that is shown in the next chapter, you will be able to determine what price you need to pay for the house in order to turn a decent profit.

Profit is the name of the game. It's no good just seeing a house that you think looks cheap. You have to see what you can compare it with. You have to see the full extent of the work needed to renovate the house and know that the price you will be able to realize will give you the profit that you anticipated within the time frame decided upon. The value of the house isn't simply what you think it's worth using guesswork. You need to be able to work the figures and be able to show your bank how you intend to make your money back, particularly if you are lending to get into the house flipping business.

Chapter 6: Requirements Of A Good

House Flipper

Following are the essentials of a good house flipper:

Excellent Credit Score: You will need a loan to go about your business and a good credit score will be helpful. Moreover, more criteria may have to be fulfilled while obtaining a loan for a high risk house flip.

Cash Availability: Availability of cash for making a down payment is an absolute must if you are buying the property through a real estate auction. If you have sufficient savings then you can hunt for a bargain-priced house and utilize your savings to pay for it. Additionally a small sized loan can be obtained for the renovations.

Knowledge of Finance Options: It is essential to be aware of the several financing options before putting your own cash into house flipping. Whether it is profitable to buy a house with cash or is a home mortgage loan better or is taking out a HELCO still better are some of the questions which need to be answered.

Knowledge of the Real Estate Market: Knowing the ways of functioning of the real estate market will be quite helpful. Which location to choose, what is the right time to buy, how to differentiate between a good and a bad deal, what will the future prospects be and many more questions have to be answered right to attain success in this business.

Negotiation Skills: You have to be aware of good negotiating strategies and also know how to tactfully bargain with the contractors and other workmen. The lesser investment you make into the property the more you earn through the process of house flipping.

Networking Skills: You should have a knack of starting conversations with potential buyers and move on to build relationships with such future buyers. This will ensure that you have a buyer ready as soon as your renovation work is completed on the house you have invested in.

Nerves of Steel: House flipping is not easy business. If all things go right then everyone is happy as is indicated in many of the TV shows on this business. But if anything goes wrong say circumstances change, and your house doesn't go off immediately then besides the above qualities it is your patience and nerves of steel that will get you past all the obstacles.

Chapter 7: Buy And Hold Property

What is CAP Rate

Your investment goals are the foundation for a reasonable CAP rate. Many financial experts find that all job and production expenses are ten percent or higher, but many are as poor as seven percent.

CAP rate is one of the easiest and most reliable approaches to assessing the merits of an investment scheme. A CAP rate is simply a function of its least simple structure to determine how many financial experts will gain and lose if they end up buying the property to which they refer. Despite the fact that a CAP rate will not give the financial experts a certain amount they still have to raise, it is also important to consider. CAP rates are no more reliable than the stock exchange forecast; they rely on a typical blunder scale and should be considered when taking into account certain factors. I reiterate the CAP rates are not 100% precise; they are used only to determine future investment benefits. All of this is important when it is accompanied by due effort and a strong focus on the properly measured value of the CAP.

CAP thresholds are not intended to act alone and should instead be used in conjunction with the various measures. A CAP rate without feedback from anyone is almost meaningless, yet a CAP rate with additional information and data will effectively reduce a financial specialist's measure of risk while making an investment. The advantage lies in finding out how to calculate high rates: the following figures can alleviate more risks than many financial experts realize. If you realize how much investment you can make, you will have a sense if you can pull the trigger in the purchase.

If you negotiate the buying and keeping of assets, usually called automated income property, with a financial expert, you will be negotiating CAP prices.

The actual capitalization rate is effectively the CAP value. It is a property's return potential for a period of one year, recognizing that the property is purchased with cash and not funded.

What cash? Here we try to standardize material. It will be difficult to analyze if you include the financial terms-of, which everyone is different. The equation is simple:

CAP rate (percent) = Market value divided into net operating revenue (NOI), which is multiplied by 100 percent.

1. Revenue= total rent. You can also check for various sources of pay that the property creates, but government leasing spots allow you to just rent regularly for 90 percent of cases for effortless purposes.

2. Expenses= property charges, condominium charges, fixes, safeguards, utility services (when you may add that to

your resident) all that you pay to maintain the property.

3. NOI= the last amount you make after all costs have been deducted.

4. Market value= asset estimate.

How important is the CAP rate?

CAP ratios are used by financial experts who choose to push a particular property forward or not. Even financial experts can be used to prepare to sell a property now and then. The highest rate for investment properties works best and cannot be as useful in various situations. For example, when determining raw ground, fixed and flip assets, and sometimes instant rentals, investors must refrain from relying upon CAP rates. This is because the CAP rate receipt is based on the annual networking pay, which in such cases is not material. Financial specialists (or even owners) may use top-rate rating when evaluating different types of properties, including

• Multifamily Rental

- Apartment Buildings

- Rentable City Homes

- Commercial

Real Estate CAP rates are relevant because they can look at the initial yield of spectra. The rates for commercial real estate CAP are large. The equation puts networking wages into relation to speculation price tags so that financial specialists can put the potential productivity of the arrangement in context. The CAP level may also indicate the time it takes for the speculation to recover. For example, it takes four years to recover the investment in a property with a 4 percent CAP rate. Overall, the CAP rate is an important way of evaluating the risk associated with a particular property for investors.

A Good CAP Rate

Each alternately interprets their ideal CAP value. Some investors use CAP in a double-digit; others are mocked by the fact that they beat placing it in a bank at a 4 percent rate.

The best question is: "How should this property norm CAP be?" Make sure you realize something that should not be uncommon, and you know if you have a DEAL. Any investment property should begin primarily by taking a look at the numbers. Although the field and conditions are important, healthy cash flow also pays the bills. Ensure that the holder collects all relevant information on current and past expenses together with current revenue. In the same way, make sure that you include the expense and replacement of the executive savings when you have a sales check, and you have everything to do with having the NOI (net operating income) for your structure. At a time when I am breaking down a property for a dealer, I accept NOI to give me a worthy sign at the supposed high rate for that type of property in an offered area. The better the income, if the CAP rate is higher. Usually, lower CAP rates are related to appeal and okay features and the opposite to higher CAP rates. CAP is a portion of the area and condition gradually compared to the number of units. Deciding a genuine ROI is more necessary, as it involves looking at the cost of funding and closing costs and is one component of an investor's cash measure that is placed alongside the holding time. In fact, ROI figures for services are to be considered.

The problem in the market today is that the demand for an MF [multi-family] property is so high that CAP rates are lower and lower, so the transient ROI, in particular, is exceptionally small or non-existent. To find a nice property you can buy and give a good ROI is now a constant challenge for all investors.

If the rental company takes care of administration, the costs will be included in your income assessment as working costs. Also, please keep in mind your income assessment for an opportunity factor. Typically this is an average gross income rate. Usually, the standard is 5 percent.

Any lease means that the tenant pays all or part of the costs of living, for instance, repairs maintenance costs or insurance to give examples. In these actions, the property owner's income is generally compensation, so normal operating costs are not taken into account as a feature of the cash flow analysis.

Towards the end of the day, your CAP gives a sense of your money.

What about CAP Rate in Real Estate Investing?

The cost-effectiveness of a land venture is an estimate used. By theory, the investment property CAP level is the property's networking expense (NOI) in accordance with the reasonably approximate value of the property.

The estimation of the CAP rate is usually taken as one way to assess the presence of an investment in the land contributing industry.

In order to measure the CAP value of a property, the networking profit is only divided by the calculation of the asset. You've got a rate to wind up. What does that really mean?

Just look at the numbers alone will not tell you the answer is better at a higher CAP level.

By comparing their networking profits with their cost (estimating the annual rate of return), the CAP rate can be used to the degree of individual property evaluation. It can also be used for the entire market by taking usual higher rates for an enormous array of real estate.

It is generally used to lease its project estate by long-term land shareholders. To assess property investment, you should use the highest rate. In any event, you may also use the CAP rate once you claim the property effectively and prior take the property to market.

Investors, shareholders, and investors buying and holding will look into the uncertainty of the CAP rate. It can be used to evaluate homes for single families, as well as homes for many families.

You may have calculated from the recipe that a higher CAP rate means either higher NOI or lower buying costs. Every investor in property cannot just accept the number for what it means and is worthwhile, although these two things seem to be extraordinary at first glance. You need to understand the higher or lower the CAP. You may be stunned to find that the high CAP rate properties you may buy are usually not the best option. Does the use of capital in investment properties provide a higher CAP rate?

CAP as Annual Rate

The annual returns are based on the calculation of the CAP rate. That includes reflecting the calculation of the CAP rate if an income property was performed well or not efficiently for one year. It suggests, though, that you will not get a glimpse at how this investment property has been working for more than a long time. This is an important part of the analysis. If the presentation of this investment property was poor in the past few years, but it did have positive returns at the time of the contract, this can be a false impression of the actual profitability of the property. In future investment tests, property financial experts, particularly amateurs, should be attentive to surprisingly high CAP rates.

Is there a trade-off in mind why we said that the maximum price for each property and a whole market could be calculated? Does a lower CAP rate boost the amount available? Given this, entire how quickly you have to start creating profits depends here. For profitable investment, you don't have to go regularly to the high-CAP regions. When you pick up a low CAP zone, in particular, after some time, the stars will be higher rates. In this case, increased NOI (lease increments combined with constant costs) is usually taken into account in the market. Despite the absence of an advantage quickly, low-CAP regions will give you long-term appreciation by increasing NOIs.

Hazard Assessment

The CAP rate is otherwise referred to as a share of the risk level of an asset. The idea is that a higher rate of CAP means a high risk of property investment, in contrast to a lower rate of CAP (usually safe property investment) in reverse. This is a similar rule that usually reveals safe resources (for example, treasury bonds) to us with low returns.

Hazard is a major part of any investment inquiry; you cannot just gander about returns. Financial experts need to examine the level of danger they are prepared to accept to defend them from cash loss. The way the property's CAP value is actually calculated is relevant to investigate. For example, a high-capacity property may not have the habitability level (which can actually affect your benefits, if they are excessively high). Or, on the other hand, a CAP ratio dependent on the numbers evaluated or the star form could be an example. Typically, CAP rates are calculated for this situation, with higher leases and fewer costs expected. Be careful when you see CAP rates for a property without input from anybody else. It's smarter to buy real rentals and costs for yourself.

Cap Rate versus ROI

For both measurements, the fundamental difference between CAP and ROI is used. As I said just now, a CAP rate for assessing the potential level of profitability (ROI) of the financial expert is used. In all things, no reason why many business people confuse both is not difficult to realize. Superficially, the two tests are basically the same: each advises a financial expert on the potential of future investment. Nevertheless, it is critical that the CAP rate and ROI satisfy an alternative criterion when a scheme is dissected. The rentability level is intended to give investors a target rate of the amount to be agreed upon. For example, ROI is usually reported as a metric to determine the potential benefit of the financial professional for his investments. Investors can thus examine the ROIs of two completely different resources. The investment rate expressed makes it easier, regardless of whether they are the same, to compare two different assets. Subsequently, finance professionals may think about the ROI for a several-month recovery by buying and holding multi-years.

In order to look at equivalent assets, the CAP value is then used again. For example, a CAP rate would be good for anyone to look at, but it is far from optimal for investors who need a turnaround and a rebound in investment property.

What is a Successful Rental Property CAP Rate?

A decent CAP rate is approximately four percent; however, it is crucial that the "decent" CAP rate should be distinguished from the "secured" CAP rate. The formula itself ties network profits to the starting price tag. Financial experts who are searching for a lower price tag will need a high CAP rate subsequently. The CAP rate of 4% or 10% could be called a "decent" investment elsewhere.

In any case, levels of capitalization have also become synonymous with risk assessment. To assess a "secret" CAP price, you must tell us how many dangers you are glad to face. A lower cap rate is generally less likely, while a higher CAP rate is riskier. Financial experts looking for a safer choice would support lower CAP properties along these lines. The main thing to remember is that, despite various estimates, you should never go out on the limb as OK with; you should use the CAP value consistently.

Core Point (CAP)

A cap level is only a way to estimate the true movement of investment in practice. Moreover, much like geology and climate examples, there are three key points that influence the CAP rate: There are three key points.

1. Financial and demographic macro-level aspects

2. Market impacts at micro-level

3. The type of property these three elements combine so that each property or regional market has its own unique cap limit. We will analyze all with a view to better understanding them.

Economic and Demographic Implications

Macro-Level CAP rate assumes that you buy a property in a major metropolis such as San Francisco. It's a big town with a strong, divergent business. It is also common because landlords and buyers are constantly flooding.

At the same time, because of land deficiencies and administrative confines, San Francisco lacks new development supplies.

Those macro-financial and demographic factors strongly affect property value, as I disclosed in the selection of the ideal location for investment properties. Most of it also reduces investor's risk to contribute their cash to the property at a site like San Francisco.

As far as CAP levels are concerned, it ensures that San Francisco has high limit rates (e.g., huge expenses). In addition, this means that speculators and property owners should, in view of the lower apparent risk, consider lower income levels for all purposes.

Again, a provincial or community market has extraordinary financial and demographic value. Such areas are not as strong financially as a new, big town with an improved economy. In this context, financial experts are calling for higher cap rates to counter this risk.

Some smaller-scale areas within the same market are superior to others.

How do Micro-Level Markets affect the Price?

In view of their area and the building condition, the business property structures are classified into four categories (A, B, C, and D).

Just keep in mind that Class A methods are the most current, best-funded, and most wanted structures, until further information. B, C, D are also progressively more and less desirable. Financial experts in each property class often qualify for distinct CAP rates.

Which Property Type Impacts CAP Rate

Suppose you buy a small property in Atlanta, Georgia. The market CAP rate for your property will usually not precisely be the CAP rate for a small retail mall (e.g., store) in exactly the same area.

Why are residential and commercial contracts? Again, this is a threat.

In any scenario, people will have to stay somewhere during a recession. This is likely to keep a loft building full irrespective of whether the rates are lower a bit.

However, during a downturn, a bloom shop leasing the retail store can leave the business. In addition, it means that the owner of the structure may face long openings and significantly lower rents.

Step by step instructions for using CAP rates as a rental investor, the option of a CAP rate may seem scholastic until now. Only a number in a report estimates a risk-like dynamic idea.

In any case, a CAP rate is a practical tool. You can use it as a financial investment property specialist at

1. To put money in

2. Choose a business, submarket, or type of property. Set goals and conduct research on real estate acquisitions

3. As a consequence, a limit level allows you to use a high calculation. In turn, great choices contribute to your ultimate goals for the land and money.

What are you looking forward to?

Your position on the future of an asset and region also depends on the "decent" CAP rate.

My opinion about this process is most likely to be inferred. I don't worry about making wagers based on a hypothesis that an investment methodology will succeed. It could be a good idea. In all cases, it still simply teaches the total and the timing of the development.

I prefer to choose markets and properties with good current CAP rates and great long-distance opportunities.

In all ways, early retirement people try to build assets and gain financial independence with income from these properties. By admitting such low CAP rates that you don't earn a salary today, your development (and a way to financial independence) is 100% dependent on external powers. I don't feel warm and fluffy inside that.

There is another factor to consider before we finish the topic of CAP rates—the cost of financing. That's something you can do little about, but it can affect both the CAP level and your overall practice.

I'm sure you've heard news about changes in the loan cost of the Federal Reserve. The rate is actually called the target rate of government support because it can impact different rates throughout the economy–including CAP rates. It is substantial. It is necessary.

CAP rates are most affected by factors such as local political, socioeconomic, and other small-scale parameters. They matter as I have clarified because they are the center of the property.

However, given that real estate appreciations rely strongly on bond funding and on domestic capital markets, the cost of loans also takes on huge work. Thus, changes in loan costs may increase or reduce the CAP rates even when the equivalent of the property or market remains.

Can the CAP Tariffs be Changed

The correct reply is YES! One thing about the property I love is that you really have a lot of control over this type of investment. One of the most important technologies in this contributing scene is "for gratitude."

Essentially, the "compressor CAP rate" is high (less costly) and lower (more costly). This is normally done through the purchase of a fixed property that buys under a rental market. When reforming it, rents that generate NOIs are increased, and the property, with some help on the renowned market, is calculated to be a success.

We come here to clean the system, to include comfort and cost as financial experts. Depending on economic circumstances, renegotiation and holding are assessed if we lease-up. When coated and performing at its maximum capacity, the property should be ordered as far as possible.

What is a Good CAP Level for Investment?

It's up to you the quick reply.

I understand that you need a stronger response to that to a greater extent, but it really depends on your own investment needs, preferences, and risk tolerance. There is no unequivocal answer, but three components are tested to choose the' decent' level: risk tolerance to explain more, how do we find two investments, one with 6% and an 8% limit?

A financial professional looking for more than one, the stable investment would find a good match between the six percent equity assets. It can be a higher value in a lower field.

A financial professional who takes more of a gamble and risk can make the 8 percent limit property a good match. It may be more upside-down but less coherent.

Controlling, I must emphasize that you can change the CAP rate, change it, and control it. Control "When you buy a 6% CAP property, it does not stay for 6% of the life of the investment, so you have to reply to this question." In reality, by efficiently increasing rents on an investment property (which generates NOI), you adjust the CAP level and increase your ROI.

The prospect of a financial expert on the ultimate destination of a certain market can also help to determine whether or not the limit price is "good." You are certain that a market has grown and know that there can be more robust reasons to buy a low-CAP asset. I really don't recommend this process, because, in every sense, it's basically betting. Basically, you wager that the market acknowledges, and you trust that the market makes your "right" investment unbelievable.

How to measure risk a CAP rate is the best understood as a measure of risk after the straightforward math retail. Thus, a higher top-level investment means more and riskier investment. A lower top-level implies a lower risk of loss.

Doesn't it mean that I am slowly at risk?

You cannot just concentrate on returns or benefits as an investor. You also have to check and make sure you have the chance to lose money.

In this respect, you can start with three central points that influence high rates to assess the risk for your investment in the property purchases more readily.

Be an expert in buying and retaining strategies. The fact that you are isolating the professionals from the rest is imaginative and knows how and when to use various strategies accessible to you as an investor. A few of the unusual deals will be the dream box of the long-term investment gained using the first FHA credit. In certain cases, while maintaining your long-haul portfolio, you should use a momentary system.

You could have skirted an exceptional grateful game on a hot market before you know that it is wrong to own a property that has no profits. You are already aware of the fact that bargains that may not cover month-to-month incentives are still earned every year on double digits. There are moments when a theory can satisfy it. This is a risky business. In such situations, an alert is key.

Similarly, the use of these transactions, and techniques for the specialist, will be protected with different types of contributing profiles, such as retailers, flippers, and property owners. Investment property arrangements are linked to the way properties are fitted into the fitting box for that particular scheme on that particular day.

No two arrangements are alike, but once you know the various techniques available both to obtain and preserve property, you will easily be able to understand which the best way of making an arrangement random is. This information is KEY as an investor to allow you and your family to continue with the creation of a rental portfolio for amazing rest.

What are Fix, Flip, Buy and Hold Differences?

The technique of correcting and contrasting was built to benefit greatly rapidly. House sales include the acquisition and rehabilitation of restricted property–such as old homes and settlements–to the profit of the buyer. Investors sometimes use temporary workers to carry out the update. Those with experienced flipping houses can take the required steps on a regular basis.

This methodology also incorporates construction value because the house loan is squared, and the house is valued. Most owners and holders typically last five years or longer before an investment property is sold for a profit.

Purchasing and keeping properties is a procedure that can make your total assets by much more than flipping your house. You can create significant month-to-month payments and a substantial benefit when you inevitably sell the property by providing ideal finance for an investment property and boosting your profits. Everything considered is not for everyone to manage the obligations and risks of dealing with a property.

Purchase and Hold Real Property Investment

There is no doubt that exceptional wealth has been accumulated. Although everyone who has been involved in the real estate sector in recent years may not think this way, it is well known that immovable value increases over time. The more you take the piece of real estate into account, the greater your appreciation potential. The absolute richest people on the planet gathered their extraordinary wealth by buying and retaining the property.

Lasting income

Owning different properties, all of which provide a strong and lasting rental pay, is a very engaging way of generating a strong salary stream. Although you can receive this equivalent kind of permanent household pay, a continuous flux of flip arrangements is required. One after the other, in general, this could be a burden or a favorable position for the low maintenance investor. It is a good sign to have a regular imbuement of cash when you properly buy, fix, and sell your home buckets. In any case, income is one of the most exciting highlights for acquisitions and property investments in order to have a strong, unfaltering, and reliable source from month to month.

Pride of ownership

I'd just drive once in a while and smile when I first started purchasing investment properties. I felt a lot about the pride of ownership. It was also great to help people who needed a decent home find an accommodating, ideal, and desirable place to live. It was also great. You have huge occupants who pay on schedules and a house that requires almost nothing, if any maintenance, and you're realizing, in addition, a clean month-to-month benefit with sound money savings.

No Need to Sell Immediately

A preferred position to purchase and hold property is that if a financial, real estate expert does not have to sell quickly, he does not have to. The purchase and holding specialists in immovable financing can withhold market downturns until economic situations improve, except if this is a serious crisis. However, if you buy the property and have ownership of the real estate, investors may be concerned about re-sales when the opportunity arrives if you acquire clean month-to-month benefits and do not need crisis support.

Simple Earning

Most of us imagine profiting while relaxing at home. Simple earning you can do this as a buy or retake investor if you rent an estate to an inhabitant who doesn't bother you. The unadulterated benefit is every lease payment that exceeds your cost. Moreover, you square off your home loan and building value as you collect leases. It ensures that you can sell the property much more than you originally paid for.

Shareholders are very good at the time of seasonal appraisal movements. A wide range of findings is available: mortgage plot, mortgage protection, and expenses for the property. Depending on the state in which you live, you can also use "green" charge credits to avoid the possibility of using sustainable energy sources.

Without twists and turns, it's your time if you buy and hold. There is always a recovery from past air pockets in the housing market, and no matter where your property is found, the odds will increase with time. In fact, the increase in investment property hold is advantageous.

Chapter 8: Choosing The Type Of

House To Flip

A house flipper must decide on the type of house he wants to flip. The house can be a foreclosure, a fixer-upper, or a new construction. It is also important to choose the right neighborhood. The house flipper must make serious research when selecting the neighborhood. He can check if there are house flippers in the area who haven't sold their house yet. He can also check the current sale prices of houses in the community. Furthermore, he can drive around the neighborhood during the day and also at night.

In flipping a newly constructed house, the house flipper has limited options especially in housing developments. Some neighborhoods may have restrictions. If the house is a foreclosed property, he will be buying the house from a lender. It is a long process that can last up to 8 months.

The internet can be a source of information regarding foreclosed homes. Fannie Mae and other lenders have a list of foreclosed houses. It is important, however, for a house flipper to examine the house first before buying it. He must not rely on pictures posted in websites.

For fixer-uppers, a house flipper can easily go out of budget. It is important for him to have an exit strategy as well as a high level of risk tolerance. In essence, it is more profitable to convert a cheap house into a nice house. Expensive upgrades don't really provide much return on investment. In renovating a house, it is better to buy materials locally. It is important not to overprice the property because buyers become skeptical in buying a home which had been on the market for a long time.

For first time house flippers, they may be encouraged to buy different properties at the same time. They fail to realize that they can easily make themselves bankrupt, especially when they use a property's equity to finance the repairs of another home. In addition, each property deserves special attention. The quality of renovation and repairs are important in selling the house.

Fixer-uppers can take a long time to finish. If the neighborhood booms overnight, there will be an increase in school improvements, local business booms, and crime rates. These factors can affect the value of the house. As such, patience is important in waiting for the community to flourish.

Chapter 9: Renovation Mistakes

Not accurately calculating the project, is the mistake people make when they are in the buying stage. Once people buy their house the two biggest mistakes people make with the renovation are not sticking to budget or sticking to the time frame – and yes you do need to have an expected time planned out. Rehabbers can increase the number of things to be done or the quality of what was planned. Even a twenty percent increase in either of these on a $30,000 project can shave $6,000 off of your profit.

It's often been said:
Plan Your Work
and Work Your Plan
Plan well, then stick to your plan. You will be glad you did. Trying to do the work yourself for most people significantly affects the time it takes to complete the project. Pay someone who can come in and blow it out. Most of the mentors who regularly flip homes will tell you that you

will make a lot more money. There are a lot of reasons for this. I get into more detail in my other book for why this is true. So we got a little bit into the mistakes people make in the restoration after the actual buying stage, but the mistake that most people make during the buying stage as they are considering a home and what price is acceptable to purchase it at, is not accurately projecting costs and not accurately projecting the time needed for the restoration.

Poor Realtor
Since your realtor will largely be handling the selling of your house much of what we say here will center on your choice of a realtor. When people go to sell their properties and they are looking for a realtor, there are a couple of mistakes I have seen people make. They hire a friend or family member, often so that person isn't offended when they find out you

listed it with someone else. I talk in my other book First Five Flips, about the difference between regarding your flipping houses as a hobby or a business. When a good CEO is considering someone for a position how much favor will he give a family member or friend for that position. What will he base his choice on, someone being offended with him? No. He or she will do their very best to find the absolute best person for that job who can help the company the most. Okay what is the next mistake people make in choosing a realtor? Someone who in their advertising flyer or brochure shows a huge number of successful sales. What is wrong with that? What if the realtor is gets those successes by persuading their clients to post very lowball listings. Why would a realtor do that when they are getting paid on commission? Okay, take a $300,000 dollar home. The selling realtor will make 3% or $9,000 in commission. What they are relying on a low price to sell your house instead of aggressively marketing it which has a cost. Let's say they get you to come down 15% or $45,000 below what good comps are suggesting. The reduction in price will cost the realtor $1,300 with no further expenditure in time designing advertising, paying photographers or layout people, not taking time to hold more open houses (they always tell you open houses don't sell houses, that they are only good for the realtor). In our experience I beg to differ with that. The realtor has also not risked spending this money on expenditures and then also taking a cut in their commission if after trying everything else they also have to lower the price. A realtor with integrity won't do this to you. They will realize that the small cut they took ($1,350) just cost their client a whopping $45,000 ! ! ! A realtor with integrity would find this unacceptable. They would also find it bad for repeat business and referrals. See if agent will give you an "Out" if you are not happy with their performance. Many agents want to "lock up" your listing for 6 months. That is eternity for a flipper. Try to make it 3 months or less. Tell them that if you are happy with what they do that you would be happy to re-enlist them but that if you are not happy you want the opportunity to make a change. On my last flip I had an awesome realtor. He put in writing that if at any time I was dissatisfied with his performance that I could terminate the relationship with no cost! Is that awesome or what? So many realtors would be afraid to do that. I wonder how much repeat business and referrals he gets because he is willing to do that. He would get one from me - I'll tell you that! Let them know what your requirements are and find one who is willing to work on that basis. It is likely that the agent will capitulate to your request. If you walk they make zero dollars guaranteed. If they capitulate, they stand to make several thousand in commissions. What would you do? Some may not go with you on this. It's okay. Walk. Better to do that than get stuck with a non-performing property that you are making payments on month after month.

What do you want to see in a realtor when you are trying to sell your house at the highest price possible? Look at their other "Sold" listings. How many have they sold in the past year? Now look at the price they got for their client. Do you see a pattern of the homes being sold way below what the other comps are? Guess what will happen to your listing? Find someone whose Sold listings are right in their with everyone else's or better. And yes, it is acceptable to ask for a list of the properties they have sold in the past year. Next are some of the mistakes poor realtors make. See if the other listings the other realtor have the following flaws.

Poor Quality and/or Number of Photos
I have seen listings with 1 picture! I can't imagine how anyone would expect to generate enthusiasm about a property with one picture. At the very least you need a nice picture of the outside front of the house. You also need a picture of the

kitchen and the bathrooms. People want to see what kind of counters you have and what kind of flooring. I've seen a lot of listings where the pictures made the house look dark inside. If the electricity is turned off a skilled photographer can still make it look bright and inviting. The average realtor is not a skilled photographer and you will be the one to suffer when the pictures taken from a "snappy" or cell phone are used to sell a house worth a quarter of a million dollars! As you go through the listings looking for properties you will see many, many, examples of what I'm talking about.

Poor or Too Brief Description of property. I have seen one line and even no line descriptions. The descriptions should include the desirable aspects of the property. It should also be worded in a way that generates excitement about it without sounding like a schlocky advertisement! Above all it should be truthful. The pictures and the description should draw, but not leave a person disappointed when they arrive at your property.

Poor people skills of selling agent. Make sure your agent has good people skills. If you don't know them very well sit in on an open house and see what they say to your potential clients. You may be pleasantly surprised, and you may be shocked.

Poor pricing. Price competitively. Going for the home run can result in a house that sits on the market too long and becomes known as a "tired" listing that will not get shown. Waiting too long before reducing price Same as above. If your realtor is getting no interest or offers you may have to consider a reduction. You do not want a "tired" listing. If the listing looks sharp, has a lot of content, you know you are priced right and in a hot enough market; if your realtor has good people and selling skills, you are at a point where you need more information. One of the best things you can do is to get the cards of the realtors who have stopped by and call them. Ask them what their honest reaction to the home was and what their clients have said about it. If you start to hear a pattern, problem solve and see how you can overcome it. If you are already in "tired" status, consider another realtor and an all new listing. Your days on the market will revert back to zero and when people look at the new pictures (make sure they are of good quality and look different than the old pictures), they won't feel like, "Oh is that thing still on the market? I've seen this thing a million times. If there is some negative defining point from the curb see if you can get rid of it. We had a property with an ugly gate in front of it. We took the gate off, trimmed some greenery, planted some flowers, put a border of those stacking stones along an unfinished asphalt driveway and it looked a hundred times better! The pictures looked different and not longer left people thinking, "Oh there's that awful one with the ugly gate." Instead they will have a positive view of the "new" house on the market and you might get it sold.

Chapter 10: Common Mistakes That

Beginner House Flippers Make And

How To Avoid Them

Along the same lines of knowing what type of repairs that you should be looking to avoid and anticipate prior to purchasing an investment property, there are also plenty of mistakes that you should be looking out for and avoiding like the plague. This chapter is going to highlight some of the most common mistakes that new house flippers such as yourself commonly make when first starting out attempting to invest in real estate. By discussing these common mistakes, the hope is that you can avoid making them yourself. Of course, there is still a chance that you will end up making these mistakes because sometimes the only way to learn is through experience; but at least this book will have been able to say, "I told you so!" if you do.

Common Property Investor Mistake 1: Using People Whom You Know as Contractors

As much as you possibly can, you should seek to look at flipping homes as a business and not like a recreational side activity that you do in your spare time. Even if you do most of your house flipping on the side when you're first getting started, you should still approach this endeavor as professionally as possible. To this end, it would probably be a good idea to avoid hiring friends or family members as contractors whenever it can be avoided. Yes, everyone wants to get that special "friend discount" when it's available, but the downside to this type of negotiation is that you as the customer will sometimes have to sacrifice quality of work in exchange for a cheaper rate. Additionally, communication paths can become murky when you personally know the person who is performing a professional service for you. So many new house flippers decide to hire friends or family members to do these people a "favor" and provide them with some business; however, in the end the investor is often left feeling as if the work was done in a less-than adequate manner or that they were taken advantage of in some way. You don't want a relationship to end because of the work that you're doing flipping houses. It's that simple.

Common Property Investor Mistake 2: Becoming Infatuated with Your Flipped Property

Emotional thinking is another huge mistake that new house flippers make, and it's one that should definitely be avoided if you can help it. When you're looking for a property to purchase that's on the market, it's extremely important that you look at it through an objective lens, rather than through a lens that is skewed towards your personal preferences for a home. For example, let's say that you are in the process of finding a property to purchase, and you find one that has an extremely large backyard. You go home and that night you dream of the potential that the backyard could yield. You think about building a fabulous outdoor patio area with a pizza oven and space for a hot tub. Then, your mind wanders to all of the friends that you could have over once that space is complete. This is an example of major problems in your thinking while purchasing an investment property.

The reality is that you and your friends are not going to be frequenting your investment property in any capacity. If you find that you're dreaming about situations where you are living inside of the investment property, then you need to take a step back and evaluate what you truly want from the property in question. Instead of thinking about how you will personally benefit from the features of the property, it's always a better idea to compare the features of the home in which you're interested with the features of the homes that surround it. If you find that you're thinking of turning the home into a grand palatial space for you and your friends or family to enjoy, you should probably consider scratching the property off of your list or taking some time to evaluate the property from an objective perspective.

Common Property Investor Mistake 3: Refusing to Seek Outside Help

It's safe to say that most if not all property investors would prefer to do all maintenance work on their own, rather than pay someone else to do it for them. Property investors by nature of their work are always eager to save money whenever it's possible; however, new investors sometimes skimp when it's inappropriate to do so. For example, if you decide that a particular bathroom in a home is in need of renovation, it would be extremely unwise of you to decide to do all of the plumbing work yourself if you have never touched a water pipe before in your life. What happens if you do the work incorrectly and a pipe bursts or the waterline stops working? There are some renovations that simply should not be done by an inexperienced house flipper, and yet many people are unable to see this fact until it's too late. Don't let yourself be one of these people; recognize when the work should be done by a professional who actually knows what he or she is doing.

Common Property Investor Mistake 4: Acting as if You Have all the Time in the World

Sure, no one is going to be watching your every move when you're flipping a house to make sure that you're sticking to a strict deadline, but that's what you have to push yourself to do! The reality is that the longer that you're holding onto a property, the more money and effort you're spending on fixing it up. The faster that you can renovate the property and get it up for resale (or rent, if that's the route you're choosing to take), the quicker you are going to see money re-enter your pocket. It might be a good idea to even set up some kind of project schedule that you can easily follow on a weekly basis. Otherwise, what you may think is only going to take one day to complete could end up costing you a significantly greater period of time.

Common Property Investor Mistake 5: Failure to Appropriately Allocate Funds

One of the biggest mistakes that a new property investor can make is put themselves into a situation where they do not have enough money to complete a project. This type of problem is a result of poor financial planning, and if this happens to you then you are going to have a hard time not only flipping the property, but also getting yourself out from under the debt that you're in. This is why recognizing the importance of a good credit score and how to calculate a home's ARV were the first two chapters of this book. If you do not do proper financial planning from the jump, you're exposing yourself to more risk than is truly necessary. Do the proper planning beforehand and the work that is involved, so that you do not ultimately end up eating the cost of a home that you so haphazardly purchased.

Chapter 11: Uncertainties And Risks

Involved In House Flipping

Market economies have unlimited uncertainties. Unlike some other businesses such as house building, house flippers are also usually unaware of the problems awaiting them behind the walls or in the inner part of ancient houses. Experience of these expose flippers to the problems that may lie ahead, and those things can be put into consideration. Most house flippers face risks ranging from interest rate risk especially those on loans to the real estate market risk.

Uncertainties have a great power to change economic decisions and increase the uncertainty of expected incomes. Uncertainties increase when there is a financial crisis or after the end of a financial crisis in a country. House flippers try their best to get make sure the house can be flipped and at a reasonable price.

Amidst all, there are various uncertainties that are the major factor which might occur just when you thought you are almost at the endpoint of the project.

These are the risk that you should always consider when you venture into house flipping.

Strategies to minimize risk and increase profitability

Market Development

Be sure of the happenings in the flipper's market, the development, and its movement. It's advisable you know if the market is favorable or set to boom flippers. Make inquiries from national sources or the local real estate agents monthly to avoid running at a loss after much work and consultations when just a phone call could have saved you from the mess.

Economy Shift

How is your economy? Is it stable or shifts with time? Is it declining or growing? You must lay your hands on all these pieces of information before you begin any deal. This will lead you on how to place your price either below or above. You have a lot of online sources where you can get these pieces of information; you are only a click away.

Rates of Interest

You need to keep monitoring interest rates. There are times when interest rates are expected to increase; therefore you must charge higher than normal to make a good profit.

Time

Although you can house flip at any time of the year, there are times you expect higher profit than other times. As an experienced house flipper, it is advisable you target those times of the year to maximize your profit. For instance, in late January, sales of homes are always low, and flippers have no choice than to sell it out at a low-profit rate to meet up loan payment. But during the middle of the year, sales rise to its peak. So, instead of flipping a house when sales are low, target and design your house flipping to meet up at the middle of the year.

Renovations Plan

Your renovation budget should outweigh the original price you are offered especially when you are on a loan. When you get this wrong, then your profit is gone, therefore, to avoid wasted effort, you must get this right and well. Make sure every renovation the house need is penned down and well inspected by professionals such as contractors and appraisers. You don't have to do irrelevant things such as the ideas of how you want your own home to be furnished. Instead, focus on the important things such as broken things and getting rid of outdated designs and updating the house to increase its price value.

Learn from Others

When you get to a crossroad and confusion sets in, don't waste time in calling the attention of your experienced friend in that field. There is a saying that "two heads are better than one" so they can always help you to get a solution to the problem instead of you trying to do more damage. This could occur in various aspects of house flipping, it could be while buying a property, rehabbing or trying to pay for commissions.

Know Your Ability

As a house flipper, know your skillset and the place where you are more comfortable to carry out your flipping business. Some house flippers are good with working with extremely old houses in a suburban setting while some can only work within not-so-old houses. Know your capability and do not exceed it to get the best result.

Contractors Problems

Even without house flipping, you can agree with me that getting a very good contractor that is also conscious of time can be quite challenging. However, to get the best out of a contractor, make sure your contract is worded consisting of the details of everything that is needed in completing the job. Do not let the contractor handle it alone, work also as a supervisor, input your own ideas too and try to correct errors immediately they are made to avoid expensive damage. When the contractor gets out of hand to refer to the written contract.

Potential to Lose a Reasonable Amount of Money

Every good thing has its own risk. Although the money you make in house flipping is mouthwatering and it comes quickly, so also can you lose a lot of money as fast as possible. These are various ways you can lose money:

Increase in tax

There is a higher tendency that the city will increase a tax on a completed property. There might be a problem if you don't get a buyer early enough therefore, you must be responsible for the payment of the tax. It can also be a hindrance to the buyer's interest in purchasing the property due to the high tax bill. In some cases, you end up losing a good part of your profit to the payment of tax. Therefore, when you own a property you are supposed to flip for over a year, your capital gain rate will vary. However, there can be a chance for you to do a 1031-Exchange and delay the taxes to a particular time in the future.

Unknown or Hidden Pairs

This shouldn't be strange to house flippers because almost all houses have this. There are times you try to remove previous doors, and, in the process, you find out the doorpost has more problem which is different from the damaged door. This is bound to happen in all homes and that leads to extra expenses especially when it was not expected. It could be a water problem on the roof or the bathroom. To avoid these problems on every repair, add a 1% contingency fee to every repair in your budget. If you do not use them, then your profit is higher but it's safer that way or in some cases, you end up spending all or some of it.

Holding Cost

The more time you are holding onto the property; the more bills you must pay. Costs ranging from the mortgage (if you have a mortgage on the property), taxes, insurance, cleaning of the environment in some cases plowing of snow. These costs swallow up the budget and make you lose more money than expected. The best solution to this problem is to sell out the property early enough but no one wants to run at a loss.

Finding It Hard to Sell Out Properties

After the buying and rehabbing of property, the most discouraging part of house flipping is not to get a buyer early enough. Every day from the day you completed the house and you couldn't get a buyer for it, you lose money. Your holding cost charges as long as the house is in your custody. When a house stays without being sold for a long period, you might eventually have to reduce its cost which will reduce your expected profit.

Stress

It is an unarguable fact that house flipping is time-consuming and very stressful. Ever house flipper must have a plan B as things most times goes beyond the stipulated times and might not even come out as planned. There are times you do the wrong things; times contractors disappoint and lots more. When you keep having experience of these things, you eventually know how to handle them when they arise again, and you won't be put off balance.

Chapter 12: Staging For A Quick Sale

Some buyers have a hard time visualizing what a house would look like and how to utilize the space, but you can provide that for them when you stage your flip. What staging does is place furnishings, artwork, and accessories both inside and outside the home to help the buyers imagine themselves living there. Here are some simple staging ideas you can do yourself to help your flips sell quicker for more money.

Stage for Your Target Market

If your flip is in a retirement area, don't stage it with a nursery or toys in a children's room. Instead, include a study or reading room with a cozy throw over a rocking chair. If your flip is across from an elementary school, chances are your buyers will have younger children. If this is the case, then include a room with bunk beds and a small desk, or perhaps a shelf with some toys or sports items. If your flip is in a neighborhood with a lot of teens, maybe you would want to include a basketball hoop above the garage or to the side of the driveway. These items would enable the buyers to imagine themselves as owners.

Your furniture should also work for your targeted market. If you believe your market to be young professionals, then stage one of the bedrooms as an office, complete with computer, desk, desk lamp, shelves, and files. Don't make the room look too crowded, just lived in and welcomed. I've even heard of investors including pet items, such as a doggie toy box and pet bowls in the appropriate space.

If your flip has a pool, stretch a net across with a ball to the side of the pool. It is inviting and fun. Also, include patio furniture and a fire pit, or perhaps a patio table and chairs to show buyers the space available to enjoy in the backyard. Make sure you have included some potted plants and groomed the landscaping, so it is clean and fresh as well.

Minimize the Bad—Accentuate the Good

Every house has its ills, and your flip is sure to be no exception. What you can do with staging will surprise you. Get in the habit of writing down what first attracted you to your flip because chances are it is an appealing feature that you can accentuate to attract other buyers. For example, if your flip has an amazing fireplace, then center the furniture around the fireplace. Place some tall plants to the side or some beautiful accessories on the mantle to draw the buyer's eye to the house's high points. If the living room has a huge picture window, don't hide the window with heavy drapes. Instead, place the furniture in a manner that allows lots of light to shine through and gives the buyers full view of the front or back yard.

If the house has a huge island, place boldly colored flowers on the island to draw the buyer's eye to the kitchen's most outstanding feature. You might also want to put some bar stools around the island so the buyers can visualize it as a gathering point in the home. If the ceilings are high with plant shelves, place a few items higher to draw the eyes to the ceiling height. For rooms that are smaller, keep the furniture to the walls so you can give the space a larger, more open feel. Avoid filling the center of the room with large coffee tables or large chairs. If the room is larger, then you can group some pieces in the corners to give the space a cozy, conversational feel. Doing so will encourage the buyers to pull up a chair and stay for a while.

If you don't want to haul heavy mattresses into the home, there are things you can do to give the appearance of a bed instead. Put up four corner stands and throw an air mattress on top. Then cover it with a beautiful spread and some fluffy accent pillows. For safety's sake, be sure to put a sign up that warns buyers not to sit or lay on the bed. In the bathrooms, put out some nice towels and hang a shower curtain for color. Put some soap dishes at the sinks and include a scented shower candle on the edge of the tub.

In the dining room, set the table and put some fruit in the center for color and scent. Turn things festive with wine glasses or cake plates. I've heard some investors say they left shoes at the front door next to a box of booties to signal they would like the buyers to take off their shoes or cover them with booties when they tour the home.

However you plan to stage the home, the spaces should be clearly defined and appropriately furnished. For example, don't put a desk in an open corner of the living room; all it does is make it look crowded and encourage the buyers to question the space. A corner lamp stand or larger plant will do the trick and not confuse the customer.

Adding Accessories

Pillows, throws, vases, trays, etc. can be added to your staging efforts to give the flip splashes of color, texture, and height. If you are staging an older home with low ceilings, don't use a lot of tall items that will draw attention to the fact that the ceilings are low and not very contemporary. When arranging accessories, there is magic in three. Three candlesticks of different heights or three pillows grouped together add balance.

Some people accessorize for aroma as well as color and balance. Scented candles, soaps, a spice rack with an opened container, or a fruit bowl with fresh oranges and lemons is perfect for color and aroma. A few books on the shelves and a pair of glasses on the side table also give the home a lived-in look.

I'm including artwork under accessories, but remember a little goes a long way. You don't want to put a lot of unnecessary holes in your freshly painted walls, so less is more. The artwork should complement the room, not dominate it. If the room is smaller and you want to give it the illusion of space, prop a large mirror against the wall and let it reflect light into the area. Just remember, going conservative on the artwork is the best.

Use your accessories to stage to the holidays or around the seasons. Use pumpkin ceramics or Christmas candles for table centerpieces. Change colors in your throws and pillows to correspond with the seasons.

Lighting is Everything

Lighting in a room can add warmth, cheer, and a welcoming feeling. Well-placed lamps and pendants will automatically draw the eye to the source of the light. Pulling the drapes and opening the blinds are a must, or just leaving everything off the windows is fine to maximize the light and open the room. Sometimes just a valance to add color and texture and draw the eye to a higher ceiling is all it takes to showcase positive features of the home.

The Challenges of Staging

The obvious challenge is where to find your furnishings, and what to do with them when the house sells. You might decide to redecorate your personal residence and use some of your pieces to stage the flip. Or, you can pick up some inexpensive furniture and accessories on Craigslist or at yard sales. Also, keep an eye out of model home sales near you; they can be a great source of inexpensive, higher quality items.

If you have no place to store your staging furniture and accessories at home, then you'll need to rent a storage space. It can get expensive to store and move the furniture to stage homes, but studies have shown that staged homes sell quicker and for more money. One investor asked a local retail tenant who had a lot of space in her store if she had room to store her staging furniture. She ended up paying a lot less and was able to keep the moving to a minimum because her store was closer to the areas where she focused on flipping houses. It helped the retailer with her lease, so it was a plus for everyone.

Most investors do not stage lower-income homes. As a rule of thumb, they tend to stage homes $200,000 and above. The lower priced homes will usually sell quickly without the hassle of staging. However, your competition is greater and so are the buyer's expectations in higher end homes.

Avoid displaying personal items like family pictures. If you have appliances in the kitchen, you might want to leave some bottled water or soda in the refrigerator and invite the buyers to help themselves. That's about as personal as you want to get.

If you decide to stage your flips, purchase smaller pieces that are light and easy to move and place. You can always group them to create weight in a room, but you cannot take bulky furniture and fit it into a smaller home. Use your accessories to give height and weight as well, creating little corner pieces that add texture and color to the room. Don't forget a few area rugs so that the sound won't echo as the buyers sit and discuss the possibilities of buying.

Most of your bigger pieces of furniture should be lighter or more neutral so that your accessories are easy to change without clashing. You can always tell when you've mastered the art of staging because buyers will begin asking you to include the furnishings with the sale. If you decide to accommodate them, make some profit on those pieces as well. A friend of mine used to stage a home complete with towels, dishes, patio, and pool toys, and several times she sold everything that along with the home. Not only did she sell everything, but she made a tidy profit from the pieces as well.

There are private companies that stage homes, just in case you have no interest in doing it yourself. Keep in mind; you'll be charged for the initial staging as well as for the length of time you keep the furnishings. Most companies will allow you to pay after the sale of the home, so that shouldn't be an upfront cost to you. The beauty of using professionals is that you won't have to hassle with moving furniture in and out and storing it between flips. If you're not planning to stage every home, this might be the way to go.

The thing that's rewarding about staging, besides the additional money and quicker sale, is that you get to see a finished product. It's a great feeling to look over the home and see just how charming and functional you have made it.

Chapter 13: Prepping The Home For

Work

Once your offer is accepted, it's not a time to stop thinking about the purchase. It's a time to up the ante and get ready for what you intended to do, and that is to program the work to be done. Establish from the real estate agent a date when you can finally have the keys and use this to create your plan of attack for the renovation. Often property investors leave things standing for a while before they program work. Any delay in the work actually costs you profit, so it's not a wise move to make. You won't need the plumber and electrician until day three of your renovation, when you have had time to assess and to clear the property of all debris. What you will need is to hire a waste skip or two and these cost money so get them from day 2, when you have had a chance to rip out any of the old fittings and fixings. You need to order this in advance usually so that it's ready for you on the day you take the keys.

The things that need to be worked out are the layout of the new home and if any walls need to come down. However you also need to know what services run through that wall and ensure that it is not a load-supporting wall. Some people start knocking down walls and are shocked to find that they support the ceiling above. If this is the case, you often have to put in beams either in timber or in metal to ensure that the support is still there. If services are located in walls that you will be knocking down, then you need an electrician or plumber to remove these.

Make yourself a plan so that you can add all the different trades to it and remember that once you agree where plumbing fittings go and where electrical points go, it's a good idea not to change your mind, so your plan will need to include all measuring up to establish where the tradesmen should fit things, especially if you are renewing bathroom and kitchen equipment. If you will be installing extra electrical sockets, these should all be marked out on the walls, so that there is no misunderstanding once the tradesmen arrive. Your planning process should follow the process set out in the following chapter.

Chapter 14: Tips And Pointers

When you are flipping for the first time, the best thing you can do is get as educated as possible. Until now, this book has been detailed about letting you know the work that goes into the house flipping process. You now have a solid foundation of knowledge on what you need to do to sell the house, but still, there is more you could know about. When you are in the industry, there is a lot you will learn along the way, this is true with anything. But you, you want to be amazing at this right off the bat, don't you? After all, who wants to face the potential of enduring costly mistakes that could have been avoided? In this chapter, you are going to learn exactly what you should know based on what others in the industry have learned. Knowing all of these tips, you will be able to make the best decisions to maximize your profits and minimize your mistakes and the length of your learning curve.

Tip #1: Assess Your Financial Situation

When you are flipping houses, you are going to need cash to do so. Earlier in this book, you learned all about financing, which is the first important step of getting a house. After all, you can't purchase a house if you aren't financially backed in order to do so! It is important you pay close attention to your financial situation and you only work within' it. For this reason, you may want to start small and then go larger as you go along. A good idea, too, if you intend to do this for a long time is to reinvest the profits into future houses. The more you do this, the more you will develop your own financial background. This will eventually eliminate the need for you to go through investors and loans because you will have your own working capital to invest.

Tip #2: Build a House Flipping Team

You don't want to have to find and hire new contractors every single time you are getting ready to flip a house. This takes up a lot of time and can be costly. It is beneficial to build up a reliable team that is going to help you make the best out of the rehabbing process and then sell your house easily. If you have ever watched house flipping shows on TV, you'll notice that they all have their own team of individuals involved. When you are building your own team, you will want to have individuals to fill the following positions on it:

Multiple real estate agents (or just one to start)

A real estate attorney

A general contractor

A designer or an architect

An insurance agent

A wholesaler

An investor (or multiple)

Having your team built will ensure that every aspect of your flipping project is overseen properly and you make the most profit back you possibly can. Having reliable individuals filling these positions will help you know you are working with the best every single time. Having your team established means they will know who you are and get to know you, and you will know who to call in every situation. It prevents you from having to go through the hiring process several times over, which saves you a significant amount of money, too.

Tip #3: Look for Undervalued Properties

You can find undervalued properties at house auctions, or through advertising yourself through "bandit signs". Bandit signs are the signs you see around town that say something such as "call "xxx-xxx-xxxx" to sell your property FAST!" You can also use e-mail marketing, mail marketing, and other means to sell your property. Having a real estate agent that consistently works with you is also a great way to find properties, as they will know when they have a lead that they can tell you about. It is very beneficial to develop a relationship with a real estate so they can help you discover properties and then later help you sell them.

Tip #4: Get Real with Your Math

The most important number to know when you are in the house flipping business is the "After Repair Value" or ARV. This number needs to be higher than what you will invest in the property so you can get a healthy profit return on the property. Your realtor will be able to decide what the ARV will be based on their estimate of the market in the surrounding area.

The next important number is the number known as the "Maximum Allowable Offer" or the MAO for short. This number describes the maximum you are willing to pay for the property.

The next part is the math part! First, multiply your ARV by 70%. Then, take away the cost of the renovations which will yield the MAO. This 70% you are multiplying in is what house flippers call the "70% rule", and it is used to help ensure your profits are maximized, and your risks are minimized. Let's look at an example below:

If the ARV you have arrived at is $100,000, then you multiply that by 70%. You get $70,000. If your cost of repairs is $20,000 in this case, then you take that away, leaving you with $50,000. That means your MAO would be $50,000 for this house. Easy, right? Doing this will save you a large amount of money in the long run by protecting you from risks and ensuring you are only investing what you know you can get back.

Tip #5: Money Likes Speed

It is important you are as quick and timely as possible when it comes to flipping houses. The faster you are, the more money you will profit. The longer it takes you, the more mortgage you must pay to hold on to the property. Therefore, the faster you are with the process, the more you will profit.

Still, make sure you are putting forward a high-quality job so you can keep your reputation clear. Your reputation will be large in this industry, and you want to be known for producing high quality and beautiful homes that people are happy to move into. The point is that they are move-in-ready; the new tenants should not have to worry about repairing any of the things you have done to the house.

Tip #6: Manage Your Finances

You want to make sure you have enough going into the project, and you want to make sure you are making a significant return. However, a common mistake that people make is they don't pay attention to their finances during the process of house flipping. You cannot simply make a budget in the beginning and assume everything is going well. It is important you track all of the expenses you put into the project, both expected and unexpected. Keeping a thorough report of this information will ensure you are staying on top of your finances and you don't run dry or eat too much into your profit margin.

Tip #7: Not Having Enough Time

When you want to get into the house flipping business, you need to make sure you have enough time to do so. While you can hire people to do a great deal of the work for you, you still need to be able to be involved in the process to some degree to ensure that everything is running properly and efficiently. If you aren't careful, you could end up with a major mess on your hands. When you are flipping a house, you need the time to acquire the house, the time to get the house inspected and do the rehabbing process, then you need to get the house inspected again to make sure it is up to code, and then you must have the time to be involved in selling it. While you can always outsource a great deal of the work, you need to realize that it will eat into your profits and you are still going to have to be involved to some degree. Before you get into house flipping, make sure you have the time to do so.

Tip #8: Having Enough Skills

You don't need to be a professional contractor to flip houses, but you do need to have some level of understanding. Or, at the very least, you need to know how to hire the right people who have the right understanding. It can be very beneficial to enter a joint venture with a partner who is skilled in the renovations department to help make sure you are buying into worthwhile projects. While you save a significant amount of money if you can do some of the contracting on your own, it isn't necessary if you want to run a business this way. Still, you are going to want to know you have enough skill to identify the right projects and get everything going so you are able to make the best of your investment.

Tip #9: Not Educated Enough

If you have read this book, then you have a great deal of knowledge needed in order to get into the house flipping business. Still, if you are not careful, you may end up getting into a situation that will cost you a significant amount of money instead of earning you a large profit. You have to make sure you really know what you are doing before you start investing large amounts of money and getting involved in costly real estate businesses. This book is a great start and has what you need to know in order to start, but you still want to make sure you start small.

If you are still uncertain about what to do or want to make sure you are being extra conservative and learning as much as possible, it can be beneficial for you to consider working together with a mentor until you are completely comfortable. Having that extra assistance can be a great confidence boost when you are getting started, and it is a great way to have all of your questions answered on the spot. You don't necessarily have to work with your mentor forever, but doing it until you are completely confident can be helpful.

Tip #10: Have Patience

Knowing that money loves speed, it can be easy to get frustrated or stressed out when you feel like things aren't moving along fast enough. It is important you have patience in this business. There is a good chance you are going to run into unexpected expenses, you are going to have to wait to get a high-quality contractor, and that there are going to be other circumstances that require you to be patient and take your time.

It is important you don't rush out and hire the very first contractor who gives you a bid you are comfortable paying, you can easily end up hiring contractors who are inexperienced or who do not produce high-quality work this way. Another thing that is important is you let the contractors have time and space to get their work done. If you are breathing down their back and stressed out, you are going to stress out your contractors, and they won't do as good of a job for you. You need to understand that sometimes you aren't going to make a major profit on every single project. The important thing is you keep going along because you need to look at the bigger picture and not become too strung out on the smaller circumstances.

The Bottom Line

There are many things you will learn when you are in the house flipping industry. This book covers a great deal of the most important information and helps you get a professional insight on the industry to help you get started. However, you are inevitably going to learn more of your own lessons along the way. The best thing you can do is be prepared to learn these lessons and take them with grace. The better you are at learning these lessons, the quicker you will learn them and the more successful you will be in the industry.

Always make sure you are looking at the bigger picture, as this business is just like any other. You are going to run into ups and downs, and you are going to learn that sometimes you have to be patient and accept that not every deal is going to be a jackpot deal. You are going to have to take your time and do your best to make sure you are fully prepared and educated when you are in the business. The more you invest in learning and knowledge, the better success you will have in your house flipping venture. And if all else fails, work together with a mentor who can teach you all of the ropes and help you feel more confident in your business venture. This will help ensure you are truly prepared to make a go of your business and make the best deals possible to maximize your success and profitability.

Chapter 15: How To Get Ahead

Awareness, networking, effort, and knowledge of the industry are all essential to success. However, it is as much about your mindset as it is about all these things. A change in your mindset can help accelerate your growth and improve your finances. Willpower and constant and consistent effort coupled with ambition can help change your mindset. You must adopt an abundance mindset if you want to be successful in life.

An abundance mindset is a change in your perception and attention. It is essentially about the resources available. An individual with an abundance mindset will truly believe that there are more than enough resources for not just themselves but others too. There is and will always be sufficient time, money, knowledge, and opportunities available. Having this mindset will help you succeed in the field of real estate investing. Here are some simple steps you can follow to develop this mindset.

Mindset About Scarcity

Scarcity doesn't necessarily have to be bad. There will be times when you might not have sufficient resources available. It might be in terms of labor, money, or even time. Instead of worrying about that scarcity, try to concentrate on things that you CAN control. Don't complain and instead take steps to rectify your situation. Complaining, whining, and moping around will not help you and will only lead to wasting more time. Instead, it is time to take action and fix the things you can.

Being Proactive

You must start anticipating and not just wait. Waiting is a passive act wherein you aren't involved, whereas anticipation helps generate excitement and expectation. When you anticipate something, you will be better prepared to deal with things. Instead of worrying about failure, wake up in the morning anticipating success. If you are flipping a house at the moment, anticipate all the things that can potentially go wrong and come up with strategies to deal with or even avoid them altogether. By doing this, you will ensure that you are always prepared and will never be caught off-guard.

Don't Procrastinate

Don't let procrastination get ahold of you. Make it your priority to do things as and when needed instead of putting them off for later. If something needs to be done now, do it immediately. You might not want to work on something at the moment, but the more you delay it, the lesser will your motivation be to get that work done.

Company Matters

The company you keep influences the way you think. When you surround yourself with motivated, passionate, happy, and ambitious people, their positive traits are bound to rub off on you too. Keeping negative company will only fester more negativity. Take some time and analyze all the relationships in your life and practically consider whether any of them are holding you back. It is better to get rid of the negative connections instead of letting them hold you back.

Believe in Yourself

At the risk of sounding cocky, it is important that you believe you are unique. No, this doesn't make you a narcissist; it is about learning to appreciate who you are and what you can do. You are a unique individual and you can use that knowledge to your advantage. Embrace your personality, both the positives and negatives. Only when you acknowledge and embrace your flaws will you be able to turn them into strengths.

Changing your mindset will take some time, and you need to work on it daily. Start maintaining a gratitude journal to make a list of all the things you are grateful for and jot down all the victories you achieve, regardless of how big or small they are. Learning to be positive and motivated will give you the necessary willpower to keep going. Spend some time listening to or watching inspirational videos like TED Talks, surround yourself with positive people, and take some time out for self-care.

Chapter 16: Steps In Rehabbing

Properties

The rehabilitation process can be divided into seven stages. The same is highly recommended in the rehabilitation business to help streamline the overall flipping process. Save time and money because it's important to have a proven system. Below is a quick list of the entire rehabilitation strategy.

Work development scope: Create a step-by-step checklist detailing exactly what the contractor should do throughout the facility.

Recruitment and contractor selection: Inform potential contractors that they are not retail customers when bringing multiple employees to bid on business.

Communicating contracts with the company: As an investor, it is important to protect yourself. Please sign the appropriate documents before starting rehabilitation.

Important documents: sign the following documents: independent contractor contract, scope of work, payment schedule, contractor insurance compensation form, W-9 tax form

Managing the rehabilitation process: In this phase, the contractor is managed through physical rehabilitation

Facility closures: Facility closures should include the final tour and final payment to the contractor.

Prepare for sale: Clean up your property as soon as possible and get ready for sale.

REPAIRED PROPERTY TYPE

In many cases, there are several categories of specific property exit strategies, as do rehabilitation. There are three main types of rehabilitation projects that investors should consider.

personal

flipping

rent

Each type of rehabilitation may propose its own independent exit strategy, but these approaches are synonymous with each other.

The same basic principles of property renovation and improvement will continue to apply. However, for each type of rehabilitation, the way in which benefits are gained is slightly different.

A good way to think about it is to think about what the ultimate goal of the renovation is. Continue reading to learn about the rehabilitation of each type of property.

PERSONAL

Personal rehabilitation looks exactly like that: the property is updated for personal use. This type of project is where the owner makes improvements for their own benefit.

They relate to functionality, aesthetics and can even increase the value of the property. Personal rehabilitation is often referred to as a simple home renovation or renovation project.

Personal rehabilitation is a good starting point for homeowners interested in moving. Owners can learn the ropes while overseeing the renovation in their home before buying and refurbishing another home.

Personal rehabilitation is a great place to establish relationships with contractors and learn about job scope and project management. An additional benefit is the ability to perform personal rehabilitation without time constraints or other stress stresses.

Flipping

This popular rehabilitation strategy involves buying a home, renovating it, and immediately selling it to make a profit. The key to a successful change is often to ensure a reasonable purchase price, complete rehabilitation quickly, and minimize maintenance costs.

When it comes to changes, time is money. Completing changes in the shortest possible time is essential to reduce asset ownership and operational costs.

Investors interested in successfully changing their homes need to make sure that they understand the local market area and how it works. This strategy also requires practical knowledge of the industry and the rehabilitation process.

A good place to start moving is to follow another investor during the process. Ask your network mentor or other investors if they can include the following contracts.

This gives you a direct understanding of the importance of a good team, a quick timeline, and a healthy market.

RENOVATION COMPONENTS

INSPECT PROPERTIES BEFORE BIDDING

Impulse buying and the purchase of "invisible" properties are at serious risk, and inspection is necessary to properly assess the condition of the property and the repair budget. This provides a clear understanding of the amount of funds required to successfully complete the project and sold for profit.

THE INVERTED HOUSE IS MECHANICALLY BAD

Focus on new paints, new carpets, floors, trimmings, kitchenware, etc., where lower cost improvements can have a major impact, and if your home has an old electrical system or the roof is leaking, rehabilitation costs is high and you spend more on.

PROFITABILITY IS PLANNED APPROPRIATELY

ROI should be calculated carefully and accurately and compared to the cost including the holding period.

PLAN DIFFERENT POTENTIAL EXIT STRATEGIES

The purpose of the flip is to make a profit immediately by selling. When spending exceeds the budget, such as raising funds or changing markets.

If you are forced to do so, a plan to hold and rent rather than lose is sometimes a better option. To do this, the purchase must be able to make money while having cash flow. If the answer is yes, it is a good purchase.

ASSUMING WHO THE BUYER IS

In addition to this knowledge, you can know the ideal price and payment amount.

You just spend money on the effort to create a product that someone in the market knows to buy.

SELECT PROPERTIES THAT CAN BE UPDATED QUICKLY

The most important rule to keep in mind when trying to turn your house over is "time is money". You must select a property that can be updated immediately and sold immediately.

Many house fins use their borrowed money to buy real estate. If you have debt, it is essential to repay the loan before interest and fines are incurred. Even if you can't borrow money to buy, quick changes are always good for business.

REACH A REPUTABLE HARD MONEY LENDER

When you find a property you want to change, it's time to purchase the house and raise money to make the necessary renovations. It is important to consider profit margins. Therefore, you should investigate your provider before you apply for a loan.

UNDERSTAND RISK FACTORS AND DEVELOP A PLAN

Changing the house is a form of active investment. A successful real estate investor is someone who understands risk factors and knows how to effectively eliminate or mitigate them.

By understanding the risks associated with entering a property, you can plan specifically how to face the potential problems and collect the resources you need to deal with difficult times.

ESTIMATE THE COST OF INVESTMENT

The first step in turning the house over is to understand the numbers. One of the most important figures is to determine the estimated cost of repair. You may need to pay real estate fees and certain closing costs.

If you borrow money to rent property taxes, utilities, insurance, interest, and a house, calculate all possible costs involved, including repair costs and other related costs.

BUILD A GOOD FIXING TEAM

Proper rehabilitation equipment is an important factor for first-time home buyers. Buyers should contact contractors and certified real estate inspectors, trusted real estate agents and mortgage lenders. Reliable contractors can accurately assess what real estate needs and repair costs.

CORRECTLY HOUSE PRICE

To change your home right away, you have to get the right price on your home when you are on the market. If you overestimate your home in an attempt to make the most money, you will simply stay on the market.

This is particularly attractive in the strong seller market when the property takes off the shelf. However, some investors suggest that you will get more money by conducting a bid war than you would get if you set the house price appropriately and overestimated.

Once you set the right price, you will receive an offer within the first two weeks and will be able to sell the house as soon as possible.

KNOW WHAT NEEDS TO BE IMPROVED

It is important to know what improvements are needed when building a house. There is a possibility of losing sales due to poor improvement of the property and increasing costs due to excessive improvement.

Be sure to check the refurbishments and repairs required for implementation and the following industry trends. If you have a budget that adds value to your home, incorporate the latest technology to improve heating, ventilation, air conditioning (HVAC), plumbing, electricity, appliances, and other smart homes.

DON'T TRY TO BE TOO BIG

Don't try to be too big, especially if you're not familiar with the fixed and turnaround business. Start with a detached house and rehabilitation for less than $ 50,000.

Similarly, purchasing large real estate at large renovation investment costs is very dangerous, especially if it has just begun. It's better to start small while learning the rope

DON'T MAKE UNNECESSARY IMPROVEMENTS

Modify only what is needed. Improving the property too much will not give you the expected return on investment (ROI).

Keep in mind that this is a business and you are not renovating the house to look like a dream home. However, this rule is an exception, for example if you are repairing and turning a multi-million dollar house and this kind of change must be impressive.

CHOOSE THE RIGHT MARKET

No, one thing is being in the right market. If you don't choose the right market, you will kill you in the first deal. Knowing the market can help in two ways. Make the right kind of updates that the market is ready to pay.

More importantly, it is likely that there are buyers waiting to purchase the final product. So do your homework and grow the area you want to turn. Since you have to travel several times a day, it is important to get close to home. You also need to select the best price range for flipping.

DETERMINE THE AMOUNT OF CASH REQUIRED

In terms of home investment, investors with little investment experience looking for hard money lenders may need to get a lot of cash. Generally, this amount ranges from 20% to 40% of sales (down payment).

However, investors can reduce this amount by negotiating a contract in which the lender acquires a portion of the profit. If investors are experienced and have a good track record, hard money lenders are more likely to support little or no private money or a down payment from borrowers.

If the investor is new and has a small amount of money, it is necessary to get acquaintances such as family and friends to promise to collect some of the money and profits. Another option is to find a wealth of business partners who will pay you while you work.

TAKE CARE OF ALL THE BIG ITEMS AND WORK CORRECTLY

An infamous stigma about house fins is that they tend to cut corners. He may sin for association, but he can give bad names to those who are familiar with their work and who are thorough. Thank yourself and take care of all important items and work correctly for the first time. Potential buyers appreciate it and create a great reputation for your company to move forward in future deals. If you cut the corner, you can bite again.

RENEWING VANITY

One of the most important improvements in repair and turning projects is the bathroom. When renewing a bathroom vanity, consider a natural colored floating vanity.

Soft and modern with rounded edges. The white quartz counter works in the bathroom. You can highlight them with a circular mirror. When selecting a cabinet color, consider shades and tones other than white. Natural nuts, mint, black and coal are successful. Sometimes white still works. Avoid shades of gray.

ADD SOME HIGH-END FEATURES TO THE PROPERTY

Try adding high-end functionality to low-priced properties. For example, you can add a wall-mounted hood when you update your kitchen. The extra charge is between $ 100 and $ 200, but it is much more expensive. This allows you to sell your home at the best price and get higher profits.

BUY THE WORST HOUSE IN THE BEST NEIGHBORHOOD YOU CAN AFFORD

"Worst" means a very poorly designed and outdated cosmetic form. Recoverable weathered hardwood, tremendous creative paint colors, disgusting carpets, unspoken scents, decades of builder kitchen cabinets, laminate or tile countertops, dirty toilets and toilets please think about it. However, make sure you have a good foundation.

Unless you are an experienced renovator or contractor, it is essential that the entire floor, roof beams, columns, beams, and critical parts of the house's structural integrity are in excellent condition.

You may get involved in transaction theft due to the doneness of the house. You are looking for a home that you can get at a much cheaper price than the cleanest and most comparable house in the neighborhood.

List all the modifications and changes that need to be made and calculate the cost of them. Subtract this from the estimated value after renovation of the house. This is a number that should not be passed.

PLAN YOUR UPDATES CAREFULLY

Planning is one of the most important stages of agreement and change. This includes interviews with contractors and subcontractors and, if necessary, conversations with engineers and architects. Secure funding sources.

Review the process, schedule, and costs for obtaining permission in the county or city you plan to change. Next, create a timeline and a general budget. These must be customized according to the properties.

INVESTIGATE THE LOCAL MARKET.

A detailed understanding of the local real estate market is important to the success of the project. For example, permission times and requirements vary widely from market to market, and requirements may change regularly.

Also, if you allow the problem, the project can be significantly delayed if not handled properly. In addition, the way you divide and categorize schools can vary widely, and knowing whether a house is in the desired school district can affect the final selling price of the house.

Proactively investigating local laws related to the real estate market and construction and comprehensive zoning can help alleviate these types of problems.

TAKE REAL ESTATE COURSES OF IMPORTANCE

Because it is important to have the right type of education at the exchange, you need to take several courses, read books, and be familiar with business and terminology.

There is a lot to learn to become a professional in the repair and transformation business, including real estate auctions, working with contractors, finding the right projects for renovation, finding the right buyers.

GET A GOOD CRM SYSTEM AND KEEP IT ORGANIZED

Learn how to get a good CRM system and use it effectively. Useful for organizing. Maintaining organization is very important in the repair and exchange business because all transactions need to be on the right track and each team member must be on time. As a result, many unnecessary conflicts and emergencies can be avoided.

FOCUS ON PAINTING, HARDWARE AND LIGHTING.

Paint, hardware and lighting are the best projects that provide ROI for home repair and turnaround. Simply update your lighting and hardware accessories throughout your home to take your flip project to the next level with minimal time and money.

FIND A PROMISING NEIGHBORHOOD

Finding a region with a bright future but cheap prices can have good results. If there is new infrastructure development in the area, it is very likely that there will be a bright future.

For example, neighborhoods that are expanding streets or building new shopping centers are growing. Make an appropriate survey on the region's future development plans and select the right region.

CHOOSE THE RIGHT MONEY LENDER

In addition to buying a home, you need money to repair the home and meet sales standards. Getting funding for solutions and changes can be difficult. Traditional lenders generally require full credit and often the process is long. It is better to find a lender that works with fins, has a simple application process, requires a small portion of the down payment, and has a quick response time.

Conclusion

Ah, the old fix and flip. It can be a very lucrative business venture. Lots of hopeful property investors have tried their hand at this exciting real estate exercise, and countless have succeeded in transitioning from their boring 9 to 5's in exchange of a life of flipping.

Is there anything stopping you from becoming a successful flipper? Perhaps the biggest obstacle in the way of any real estate rehab beginner is the fear of striking out. Any sort of apprehension, anxiety, nervousness, or fear can cause you to make the wrong decisions along the line, crippling your profit and causing your venture to crash and burn.

If there's anything you need to take away from this guide it's that house flipping needs your whole confidence and resolve. You need to be dedicated, you need to be committed, and you need to be aware of the risks in order to make sound decisions even during times of potential failure.

Will you fail? Let's be real - you might. That's a danger that you have to face. But if you're brave enough to see it through, you might just be staring at your next million-dollar enterprise.

So, to set you off on your way to your first flip, take these words from Giovanni Fernandez, the owner and CEO of National Real Estate:

Remember, there are risks and potential downward spirals in every market. You get ahead by choosing a market that poses the least risk while offering the most gain.

When you flip houses, you're essentially buying and owning properties for short periods of time. And anyway you look at it - homeownership is an asset. As long as you have land, you stand the chance to make a profit. And that's a very powerful place to be.

Now, go, humble house flipper. And find your first profitable property in the great beyond.

CPSIA information can be obtained
at www.ICGtesting.com
Printed in the USA
LVHW020741230421
685284LV00017B/750